Welcome to Philosophy!

A Handbook for Students

TITLES IN PHILOSOPHY

Ayer, Sir Alfred J. · Oxford University · *The Origins of Pragmatism—* Studies in the Philosophy of Charles Sanders Peirce and William James

Ayer, Sir Alfred J. · *Metaphysics and Common Sense*

Baum, Robert J. · Rensselaer Polytechnic Institute · *Philosophy and Mathematics*

De Lucca, John · Queen's University · *Reason and Experience*—Dialogues in Modern Philosophy

Ginsberg, Robert · The Pennsylvania State University, Delaware County · *Welcome to Philosophy!*—A Handbook for Students

Hanson, Norwood Russell · *Perception and Discovery*—An Introduction to Scientific Inquiry

Hudson, W. D. · Exeter University · *Reason and Right*—A Critical Examination of Richard Price's Moral Philosophy

Humphreys, Willard C. · Evergreen College · *Anomalies and Scientific Theories*

Ross, Stephen David · State University of New York, Binghamton · *Moral Decision*—An Introduction to Ethics

Ross, Stephen David · *In Pursuit of Moral Value*

WELCOME TO PHILOSOPHY!
A HANDBOOK FOR STUDENTS

ROBERT GINSBERG

THE PENNSYLVANIA
STATE UNIVERSITY

FREEMAN, COOPER & COMPANY

SAN FRANCISCO, CALIFORNIA · 94133

Acknowledgments

Grateful acknowledgment is made to the following for permission to quote copyrighted material: The Bobbs-Merrill Company, Inc., for René Descartes, *Discourse on Method*, trans. Laurence J. Lafleur, copyright 1950, 1956. Dover Publications, Inc., and Sir Alfred Jules Ayer for *Language, Truth and Logic* by Alfred Jules Ayer, no date [1936?]. Dover Publications, Inc., for Clarence Irving Lewis, *Mind and the World-Order*, 1956. Daniel D. McGarry for *The Metalogicon* of John of Salisbury, trans. Daniel D. McGarry, copyright 1955. Oxford University Press for Aristotle, *Nicomachean Ethics*, trans. W. D. Ross from *The Oxford Translation of Aristotle*, ed. W. D. Ross, Vol. IX, 1925, and for Paul Tillich, *Love, Power, and Justice*, 1954. Princeton University Press and the American-Scandinavian Foundation for Søren Kierkegaard, *Concluding Unscientific Postscript*, trans. David F. Swenson and Walter Lowrie, copyright 1941, © 1969. Random House, Inc., for Thomas Aquinas, *Introduction to Saint Thomas Aquinas*, ed. Anton C. Pegis, copyright 1948.

This book incorporates material from *Introduction to Philosophy* by Robert Ginsberg, published by the author in Philadelphia and copyright,© 1970, by Robert Ginsberg.

Contents

Welcome to Philosophy!

A Handbook for Students

Dedicated to the 2,146 students who have taught me.

Greetings

Welcome to philosophy. This book is designed to help in your beginning acquaintance so that you and philosophy will get along on better terms. It is not *about* philosophy, but introduces you to undertakings that *are* philosophy. You will have to find out what philosophy is by participation.

This is a practical book; you will be doing the practice. There are suggestions and reminders about how to proceed and what to avoid. The book has been kept short, simple, and handy so that you will find it easy to use. Make it a helpful companion throughout your course-work in philosophy.

The chapters treat the principal features of philosophic work as undertaken in college courses. Each chapter begins with what you are likely to be troubled by, then leads to what I would like you to be troubled by. Where appropriate the chapters are complemented by passages for study. The passages selected from important philosophic texts are not proposed as authoritative answers but as stimuli to your thinking. The comments by students are drawn from a decade of course evaluations.

I try to give you hints that will make philosophy work well for you (i.e., make you work well philosophically) no matter what the institution, who the instructor, or when the course, but as a practical matter you will have to take account of the special circumstances and requirements of your own classroom encounter. Not all beginning courses in philosophy are the same. Indeed, no course is the same as any other, since different instructors and different students create different intellectual events. *Your* course in philosophy, then, is unique. Hence, there is an inherent limitation to the advice given here, for it cannot fully apply to the particular experience of philosophy you are undergoing. Each instructor will have his (which stands for "his" or "her") preferences as overriding alternatives outlined here.

Frequently, we will mention *the student's responsibilities.* They don't simply mean the tasks required of you for credit in a course, but refer to your intellectual responsibilities—that is, what you ought to require of yourself as a person engaged in the full and fair use of your intellectual powers. To be the responsible party in this sense is to be the only one who can answer to your needs, for only you can use your mind.

Chapter 1 discusses philosophy as a *discipline* of thought in such a way as to distinguish it from other disciplines that are more familiar to you or that you might encounter in college. In Chapter 2 we see how philosophy thinks about the main areas of problems which constitute its *branches*.

Philosophic coursework generally begins with readings as the occasion for thought and the subject for discussion and lecture. Chapter 3 illustrates what to look for when *reading* works of philosophy. Reading, discussing, and writing philosophy are all dimensions of thought, each with its own procedures. But there are also some general features of *philosophical reasoning* that are explained in Chapter 4. Reading, discussing, and writing philosophy require special care in the use of *language*. Chapter 5 explores the requirements of philosophical language and includes a Glossary.

Chapter 6 discusses philosophic *writing* in general as well as the preparation of term papers. Chapter 7 considers *examinations* as a special learning experience in philosophic writing. It contains a sampling of actual exams. In Chapter 8 we explore the use of the *library* for philosophical purposes, including work on term papers. You will find notes on all the thinkers mentioned in this book in the Biographical Notes.

This book has gained its shape and substance in response to student needs. You who use it have a hand in its possible success and you are the best measure of its failings. Your suggestions for improving it in the light of your work in philosophy will be appreciated by the author and eventually by future students. Please send your complaints, examples, queries, or comments to the author in care of the publisher. A clip-out sheet is included in the back of the book for your convenience.

Thank you for letting me work with you.

R. G.

1

What Philosophy Is . . .
and Isn't

Unfamiliarity and expectation. *Philosophy is a subject you probably have not yet studied.* Before studying something new it is appropriate to envision its nature, its purpose, and its procedures. What, then, *is* philosophy? You probably would like to be told the answer. Indeed, you may be expecting college to answer all your questions. But you already have some thoughts about philosophy, since you are now taking a course in it, and you might just as well begin with the possible answers that come to mind. In college you are expected to formulate and pursue important questions, not just receive answers.

What do you think philosophy might be? If you elected to sign up for a philosophy course, why did you do so? If you are required to take the course, why do you think it is required? You have ideas about science, history, religion, and literature; what do you think philosophy could be that makes it differ from these fields? You may get an idea of philosophy by contrasting it to other subjects that you have already studied or have a clear idea of. In this sense, you can get a good initial grasp of what philosophy is by seeing what it isn't.

Doesn't everyone have his own philosophy? But if that were the case why should anyone study what he already possesses? Perhaps what we mean in saying "everyone has his own philosophy" is that everyone has his own unquestioned convictions and prejudices. As philosophers, we are called upon to question beliefs and support judgments. That we have a set of favored opinions does not mean that we have a philosophy.

A quick answer to the question, "What is philosophy?" can be had by consulting your textbook, looking in a dictionary, or asking someone who took the course last term. But what will be the worth of that single answer? There are many textbooks, many dictionaries, and quite a few students. You will have to make sure that the authority you consult gives a correct answer. But that means you will have to find out what philosophy is in order to judge what you are told it is. Finding out what it is means much more than hitting upon a one-sentence formulation. You will come to learn what philosophy is by engaging in it. *Philosophy defines itself by use,* and it is you who must put it to use. What can now be offered to you are some guidelines for use.

Discipline.   Philosophy is not a body of knowledge. It is a *discipline*. It is not an organization of the facts in some field but a set of skills relevant to all inquiry and assessment. The chief significance of a discipline, such as philosophy, is in formation of the mind, not information of the mind.

You are no doubt studying other disciplines in college, such as science, mathematics, and history, though you may think of them as *subject matters*. Courses in these fields can be taught with a dual purpose: to acquaint you with the chief facts arrived at in a particular field and also with the chief ways of thinking appropriate to each discipline.

Formal courses are often only samples or models of what you can do. To fully profit from such courses you should extend and apply their concerns outside the classroom. What goes on in the class is the tip of the iceberg; the rest awaits discovery by the explorative mind on its expedition beneath the surface. A course is an occasion for self-exertion. It is a limited time for concentration of your skills in selected ways. It is a carefully organized effort to get you to do certain kinds of work. A course is a sequence of learning in which what happens in the last weeks may be quite different from what occurred at the start. This is not simply a matter of knowing more but of understanding better. A student commented on philosophy: "The value of this course came not in the classroom but outside, where I constantly found myself questioning arguments learned in class."

College offers you more than facts without thinking. In some courses, including philosophy and mathematics, thinking may be primary while the facts are few or ordinary. Thus, courses differ not only in terms of their subject matter but also in terms of how they study their subject matter.

Subject matter.   A first question often asked of philosophy is, "What is it *about?*" But the answer may prove troubling to you, for philosophy is not about any subject in particular. It has no fixed subject matter as does, say, botany, which is about life in the plant realm. Philosophy is unlimited in subject matter. There is no stopping it. It may be relevant to all fields of knowledge and human activity. Thus, *philosophy is universal in subject matter*. It may deal with the universe, with you, and with anything else of importance.

In this respect philosophy is akin to the arts, for painting and literature may explore any subject under the sun. The arts can entertain by means of imaginative creation. Philosophy aims at truth by means of reasoning. Yet the experience of art can reveal truth to us in a moving and full-bodied way, and philosophy may prove an entertainment to the intellect.

> "Beauty is truth, truth beauty,"—that is all
> Ye know on earth, and all ye need to know

says the poet Keats [*Ode on a Grecian Urn*, verses 49–50]. The philosopher seeks to know more by *the use of reason*.

Problems in philosophy.   Philosophy is the reasoned examination of fundamental and disputable *problems* in an effort to understand them in their fullness and to resolve them as best we can. Philosophy is an art of responding to intellectual problems, an art of probing what is important and difficult. *Philosophy is an open experiment in rational thought by a being that lives in a world of problems.* All fields of knowledge and practice deal with problems. Problems in philosophy are dealt with in ways somewhat different from those in other disciplines.

Technical vs. fundamental.   Each discipline faces two kinds of problems: *technical* ones which can be dealt with on the basis of what is already known or assumed in the discipline, and *fundamental* ones which challenge the very roots of the discipline and test its outer limits. Each course you undertake in college will have a mixture of the technical and the fundamental. Most disciplines attempt to transform their fundamental problems into technical ones. Progress consists in regularizing problem-solving and increasing the scope of answers generated by the body of knowledge. Such disciplines may probe fundamental problems and cause upsets, but they often have a conservative side in that they avoid rocking the boat of knowledge they sail on.

Radical discipline.   Philosophy is different. It is more of a *radical discipline* which constantly seeks out the roots of knowledge and raises challenges about what we think we know. Philosophy is an art of rocking the boat. It establishes fundamental problems where we thought technical procedures would suffice. *Philosophy increases the scope of our wondering.* It pursues what is strange until it becomes familiar, and it re-examines what is familiar until it becomes strange. Philosophy is a practice of discovery that often requires us to be somewhat at a loss.

Philosophy can become a highly technical operation in which detailed applications are made of some presumed principles or accepted methods. Excess of technicality is a chronic ailment of philosophy. May you escape the disease.

Answering and questioning.   You may think of your college work as accumulating knowledge. But a good part of your work must be explorative and evaluative rather than accumulative. Philosophy does not concern itself much with amassing a quantity of factual knowledge, though it does seek improved understanding. "Much learning," warns Heraclitus, "does not teach understanding." [Philip Wheelwright, *Heraclitus* (New York: Atheneum, ".Atheneum Paperbacks," 1964), fragment 6, p. 19.] In philosophy we may even have to give up some of what we have taken for knowledge in order to know better. A student once told me, "I learned how I think as I unlearned what I thought." Too often we learn the answer to some problem without really understanding the problem; the right answer seems to save us the trouble of thinking. In philosophy we may reach a greater understanding of a problem even if we do not settle what the right answer to it is.

The first response of the philosophic spirit to any problem is to question rather than to answer. We may question others (as did Socrates in dialogue), we may question books (as did Aquinas in commentary), we may question ourselves (as did Descartes in meditation), we may question nature (as did Francis Bacon in induction). Your experience of questioning in the classroom may have taken two forms: the instructor asking questions which you are expected to answer; you asking questions which the instructor answers. In the one case the instructor checks to see if you have the right answers; in the other case he provides them for you. That is not what is meant by *philosophic questioning.* The latter takes place when both the instructor and the student question the available answers.

Distinctive discipline.   Philosophy, then, is rather *unusual* among the higher activities of the mind. It has second thoughts about what other disciplines might not think much about, for they must make certain commitments in order to pursue the studies that are the province of their particular field. While other fields do re-examine their basic commitments from time to time, philosophy seems to spend most of its time in such re-examination of itself. Philosophy considers inquiry into the foundations rather than acquisition of information to be of first importance. This does not imply that other fields are trivial or lack an interest in fundamental pursuits. What is fundamental changes with the perspective of each discipline. Philosophy has no clear limit on subject matter. While we do not at present have a philosophy of garbage-collecting, it is conceivable that one will be worked out. Indeed, those working on problems of social justice or constructing utopian societies should give some consideration to this neglected area.

We can now reach a clearer understanding of how the work of philosophy is distinguished from other fields: (1) Philosophy treats some problems that seem to belong to other fields. Philosophy has areas of overlap with other subjects, though it does not encompass all their aspects. (2) Philosophy treats problems that seem too large or fundamental to fit any other single discipline. Several fields may do excellent—though quite different—work on a great problem, and philosophy helps out by integrating our understanding of the problem. (3) Philosophy treats other fields as themselves constituting problems.

Looking at other disciplines.   As an example of the first relationship consider this problem: *How* do you know something? The science of psychology provides answers by treating learning as a kind of behavior which can be observed and experimentally tested. But the philosopher looks over the shoulder of the psychologist and raises troubling questions about the problem, such as, "What is knowledge?" "How do I know when I know?" "How do you know when I know?" "Does either of us know?" Before you know it, the questions of philosophy have outstripped the answers of psychology. This does not belittle the work of psychology as a science, nor does it invalidate its answers. Rather, philosophy leads us into a different kind of work on the problem. Incidentally, psychology was originally a branch of philosophy dealing with mind, but at the turn of the century it developed into a separate discipline, making use of experiment and observation, and extending its field to all forms of animate behavior.

Crossing disciplines.   The understanding of knowledge is a challenge for several fields, for there seem to be forms of knowing dealt with in literature and art courses, in religious studies, even in mathematics. It has been claimed that there are forms of undemonstrable knowledge.

Faith, intuition, and aesthetic apprehension may be such forms of knowing. Philosophy will explore these possibilities as it seeks the fullest understanding of human understanding. Philosophy studies the kinds, the criteria, and the limits of knowledge.

Apparently philosophy concerns itself with minding the work of all other disciplines. Where other disciplines fear to tread philosophy enters in with daring (some would say foolhardiness). Philosophic issues which are too large for an individual discipline are the meaning of life, the purpose of the universe, the substance of reality, and the identification of justice. These may prove too large even for philosophy. Philosophy in turn can become a subject matter studied by other disciplines. Thus, the historian of the American Revolution might well consider the political theory of John Locke, while the literary critic working on the novels of Dostoyevsky and Tolstoy might well consider their theories of individual, society, and history.

Seeing the limitations of disciplines.   Philosophy examines the assumptions and methods of each field of knowledge, the structure of its principal theories, the inherent limitations and the full potentialities of the discipline. Philosophy also relates, compares, balances groups of disciplines and large areas of human knowledge and endeavor. What is the value of the arts to man? What do science and religion have to offer and can they be compatible? What is the proper structure for society? What is a human being? Philosophy is a license to cross all disciplines in pursuit of the truth concerning the greatest questions. Thus, all of your college education may come within the purview of this comprehensive and integrative discipline. You may use it to examine the roots of what you know and to connect the several areas and concerns of knowledge. Hopefully, philosophy will help you to appreciate the accomplishments and potentialities of fields other than itself.

If philosophy explores the limitations of all other branches of knowledge, what field explores the limitations of philosophy? Philosophy. Self-criticism is the inevitable and crucial responsibility of philosophy. Philosophy is *a reflective art:* it bends back and thinks twice about things, including itself. In philosophy there is always room for ifs, ands, and buts,

Controversy.   Philosophy is an art of *fruitful controversy*. It challenges claims that are established and it re-establishes claims that have been challenged. What philosophers affirm or deny may startle and disconcert. Among the strange claims and arguments you may encounter are:

The principle of all things is water (Thales).
Everything flows (Heraclitus).
Man is the measure of all things (Protagoras).
No man voluntarily does evil (Socrates).
No child can be happy (Aristotle).
Things are ideas (Berkeley).
God is dead (Nietzsche).
We are condemned to freedom (Sartre).

Philosophers have debated with themselves whether matter exists, whether God exists, even whether they themselves exist. One philosopher who debated these questions, Descartes, confessed, "I had discovered in college that one cannot imagine anything so strange and unbelievable but that it has been upheld by some philosopher; . . ." [René Descartes, *Discourse on Method*, trans. Laurence J. Lafleur (Indianapolis, Ind.: Bobbs-Merrill, "Library of Liberal Arts," 1956), Pt. II, p. 10.] If at times the questions as well as the answers of philosophers sound fantastic, do not let that keep you from seriously measuring their contribution to truth. Do not be upset when one philosopher asserts what another denies, and vice versa. What matters is that you examine the clash of arguments about a controverted point, for this provides an opportunity to discover the truth. As Condorcet said of Descartes, "The very boldness of his mistakes served the progress of the human race." [Condorcet, *Esquisse d'un Tableau Historique des Progrès de l'Esprit Humain* (Paris: J. Vrin, 1970), 8th Epoch, p. 144.] Many of the views read or discussed in philosophy may well turn out to be wrongheaded, *but there is a value in studying what is wrong.* John Stuart Mill counts this benefit as "the clearer perception and livelier impression of truth, produced by its collision with error." [John Stuart Mill, *On Liberty* (New York: Appleton-Century-Crofts, "Crofts Classics," 1947), p. 16.] So important to the understanding is the conflict of error with truth that Mill argues:

> . . . if opponents of all important truths do not exist, it is indispensable to imagine them, and supply them with the strongest arguments which the most skilful devil's advocate can conjure up. [*Ibid.*, p. 37.]

Philosophy requires a broad exchange of views, a willingness to discuss differences with others, tolerance for the unpopular, skepticism for the accepted, self-criticism for one's views, and respect for others concerned about the truth.

Making problems. Philosophy is a creative art of making problems. It may find them where other approaches detect none, it may gather them from the partial treatments given in other fields, it uncovers them for the direct work of our intellect. *Philosophy probes problems.* It tries to show *what* a problem is in the sense of what is problematic about it. It explores the alternative possibilities of dealing with the problem.

In other fields you may be encouraged to identify the right answer in a dispute and discard the other answers. But in philosophy answers are not immediately identifiable; that is often what makes the problem a philosophic one. Moreover, there may not be a single right answer. A number of alternatives may be valuable in different ways. And considerable attention to the wrong or inadequate answers may be philosophically helpful in pointing the way to what would be desirable in a proper answer. Some problems are worth study whether they have right answers or not.

Confusion. At this point you may feel some confusion about philosophy. Confusion does not spell defeat of the intellect, for the intellect may be the very power to dispel confusion. *Warning:* you will have to bear confusion, frustration, and doubt if you are to philosophize. Otherwise you will miss the very difficulties that philosophy is called upon to meet. It is important that you learn to bear confusion in your intellectual life and develop the ability to respond constructively to it. Occasional confusion is intellectually healthy.

As you begin to explore a philosophic problem you may detect an unexpected elusiveness to it. Philosophy seems to push out of your hands each solution you reach for. As you look about, you see a number of different possibilities, some in opposition to each other. Richness of alternatives can be intellectually confusing, especially if you have been habituated to receiving the authorized answers. Confusion, doubt, and lack of knowledge ought to be viewed as incentives to learning, for they can stimulate us to clarity, inquiry, and knowledge. Carefully examine what precisely it is that confuses you; formulate what the difficulty is that you face. This is a first step in mastering the difficulty and advancing understanding. In the first weeks of an introductory course in philosophy, the class complained in unison, "We are all confused!" "Good!" replied the instructor. "You have made a fine beginning."

Difficulty. Philosophy is not easy work. It makes difficulties for itself. In philosophy thought (Lat.: *cogitare*) is often agitation (*coagitare*). When you have mastered difficulties and are having an easy time of it, that is the time to move on to more difficult work. *Philosophy progresses in difficulty.* Philosophy enriches difficulties. Difficulties enrich philosophy. The consolation is that when you look back over what you have done you will be struck by its simplicity in comparison to what you have yet to do. Philosophy often advances in spiral fashion: as it moves on to new difficulties it throws new light on problems left behind. Those who always flee intellectual difficulties don't know what they are missing: the full development of their intellect. Remarking upon the hardships of reaching peace of mind, Spinoza says, at the close of his difficult masterpiece on *Ethics:* "But all noble things are as difficult as they are rare." [Benedict de Spinoza, *Ethics,* trans. William Hale White and Amelia Hutchinson Stirling (New York: Hafner, "Hafner Library of Classics," 1955), Pt. V, Prop. 42, note, p. 280.]

A philosophy course is a planned succession of obstacles designed to develop your rational skills. Even as you complain that you are getting nowhere, you are affirming your skills of judgment and inquiry. Thus, be prepared to undertake your course in philosophy as a develop*mental* experience in which you think about matters that you didn't know could be thought about. *You do not quite know what you will come to know.* In higher education learning is usually accompanied by frustrations and surprises.

Criticism and evaluation. Philosophy is a *critical and evaluative discipline.* It tries to decide issues, to judge proposed resolutions, to weigh one position against another, to discover faults in reasoning, to discover insights in arguments, and to arrive at the most defensible conclusion. Thus, though philosophy is reflective, tolerant, and pluralistic, it also moves toward settlement of what is in dispute. *Philosophy invites us to take a stand.* Not any old stand, but a stand upon firm grounds that we can argue for. Don't let the controversy pass you by without your getting into it. Don't get into the controversy without trying to get out of it by settling it. Philosophy is not merely the work of others, even when you study the work of others, for your judgment must always be put to the work. If you do not resolve the problem, who will? If not now, when? If not here in college, where?

Philosophy requires that we exercise our judgment. We have to clarify our values and also evaluate them. To evaluate something is to advocate the values one applies. Philosophy is constantly assessing and arguing.

Inquiry and argument. Philosophy is the discipline of reasoning. There are two sides to such reasoning: inquiry and argument. *Inquiry is the art of exploring problems;* it is a questioning. *Argument is the art of* *advancing reasons;* it is a constructing. We may question our arguments and we may offer reasons for our inquiries. Philosophy in these ways reflects upon itself. It corrects itself and advances itself. Philosophy is the adventure of your intellect in its encounter with itself.

Life.   Philosophy is after more than knowledge or understanding; it is the pursuit of wisdom. Wisdom is knowing how to live well. Pythagoras had a word for such a pursuit: *philosophia,* "affection for wisdom." Socrates engraved into the Western consciousness the vision of the philosopher as lover and seeker of wisdom, distinct from those who pretend to be wise and to dispense wisdom, the sophists. There is a connection between philosophy's quest for better understanding and its hopes for better living. In the last analysis, the intellectual activity of philosophy is a conduct of living. The discovery of truth, as well as the failure of our efforts to discover the truth, have consequences for our lives. Jesus told his listeners, "Ye shall know the truth, and the truth shall make you free." [*John* 8:32.] As philosophers *we shall try to know the truth by every effort of our reasoning minds,* and this trying may make us free as thinkers upon the earth. Philosophy is not a mere game, though it has its playful and entertaining features. Philosophy is not exiled in the realm of ideas, for ideas inhabit the world.

Karl Marx complained, "The philosophers have only *interpreted* the world, in various ways; the point, however, is to *change* it." [Karl Marx, "Theses on Feuerbach" in Marx and Engels, *Basic Writings on Politics and Philosophy,* ed. Lewis S. Feuer (Garden City, N.Y.: Doubleday, "Anchor Books," 1959), Thesis XI, p. 245.] Yet Marx missed the insight that philosophy does change the world, for to interpret the world correctly is to change oneself. Philosophy can aid one to become oneself. To set yourself in order is to begin a revolution of the world. The importance of philosophy lies not in the bookwork and the intellectual exercise but in the fruits of a full and responsible life. Such consequences are rarely mentioned in the classroom. They constitute the private dimension of your work, and you are only working on the roots for future growth. But as you proceed in the coursework and even after it you should give thought to what philosophy could mean to you and to what your life can be.

If philosophy does not profess to possess wisdom but only to seek it wherever it may be found, then there is no assurance of success. Philosophy is always a risky business. The truth and the good life may elude us. Let that not be because we fail to put our minds to finding them. Who enters the door of philosophy passes under a warning sign:

No Guarantees.

Philosophy is an act of intellectual courage. Take courage, for you have entered.

Passages for study

1. For, as we have seen, the function of the philosopher is not to devise speculative theories which require to be validated in experience, but to elicit the consequences of our linguistic usages. That is to say, the questions with which philosophy is concerned are purely logical questions; and although people do in fact dispute about logical questions, such disputes are always unwarranted. [Alfred Jules Ayer, *Language, Truth and Logic* (New York: Dover, no date), p. 133.]

2. Philosophy, if it cannot *answer* so many questions as we could wish, has at least the power of *asking* questions which increase the interest of the world, and show the strangeness and wonder lying just below the surface even in the commonest things of daily life. [Bertrand Russell, *The Problems of Philosophy* (New York: Oxford University Press, "A Galaxy Book," 1959), p. 16.]

3. This is a very different course, in that *we* have to provide both questions and answers. It's frustrating and provoking. [Student comment.]

4. I had some difficulty adjusting to the philosophic way of thinking at first, but found that questioning accepted ideas is a much better way of thinking than believing anything told to you. [Student comment.]

5. It is—I take it—a distinguishing character of philosophy that it is everybody's business. The man who is his own lawyer or physician, will be poorly served; but everyone both can and must be his own philosopher. He must be, because philosophy deals with ends, not means. It includes the questions, What is good? What is right? What is valid? Since finally the responsibility for his own life must rest squarely upon the shoulders of each, no one can delegate the business of answering such questions to another. [Clarence Irving Lewis, *Mind and the World-Order* (New York: Dover, 1956), p. 2.]

6. It seems then the true theories are exceedingly useful, not only as the means of knowledge but as guides of life; for as being in harmony with facts, they are believed, and being believed they encourage people who understand them to regulate their lives in accordance with them. [Aristotle, *Nicomachean Ethics*, trans. J. E. C. Welldon (London: Macmillan, 1892), Bk. X, ch. 1, 1172^b, p. 316.]

7. To be a philosopher is not merely to have subtle thoughts, nor

even to found a school, but so to love wisdom as to live according to its dictates, a life of simplicity, independence, magnanimity, and trust. It is to solve some of the problems of life, not only theoretically, but practically. [Henry David Thoreau, *The Variorum Walden*, ed. Walter Harding (New York: Washington Square Press, 1971), p. 10.]

Bibliography

Boethius. *The Consolation of Philosophy*, trans. Richard Green (Indianapolis, Ind.: Bobbs-Merrill, "Library of Liberal Arts," 1962).

DeLucca, John. *Reason and Experience: Dialogues in Modern Philosophy* (San Francisco: Freeman, Cooper & Company, 1973).

Dewey, John. *Reconstruction in Philosophy* (Boston: Beacon Press, "Beacon Paperback," enl. ed., 1964).

James, William. *Some Problems of Philosophy* (New York: Longmans, Green, 1911), Ch. 1.

Johnstone, Henry, Jr. (ed.). *What Is Philosophy?* (New York: Macmillan, "Sources in Philosophy," 1965).

Maritain, Jacques. *On the Use of Philosophy* (New York: Atheneum, "Atheneum Paperbacks," 1965).

Merleau-Ponty, Maurice. *In Praise of Philosophy*, trans. John Wild and James M. Edie (Evanston, Ill.: Northwestern University Press, 1963).

Nietzsche, Friedrich. *Beyond Good and Evil*, trans. Helen Zimmern, *The Philosophy of Nietzsche* (New York: Modern Library, 1954), Ch. 1, "Prejudices of Philosophers."

Ortega y Gasset, José. *What Is Philosophy?*, trans. Mildred Adams (New York: W. W. Norton, "The Norton Library," 1960).

Plato. *Apology*.

———. *Republic*, Bks. V–VII.

Unamuno, Miguel de. *Tragic Sense of Life*, trans. J. E. Crawford Flitch (New York: Dover, 1954).

2

The Branches of Philosophy

Philosophy courses are generally arranged as studies within one or more areas or *branches* of philosophy. The basic introductory course may cover, in a most selective way, as many as half a dozen such branches. The principal branches are surveyed here with an indication of their problem areas. This chapter may help you identify the scope of your course. However, if you want to get right down to the work of philosophy, skip this chapter. You can return to it later if you are curious about the content of other courses in philosophy.

Metaphysics.   When we direct our inquiry to first principles, we ask questions such as, "What is the universe made of?" "What holds it together?" "What started it going?" "How does it operate?" "What purpose or meaning does it have?" "What place do mind, soul, and will have in the workings of the universe?" These are rather large questions, and large questions are fit subjects for philosophy. You have thought about some of these questions before. They may have dazzled your mind or left you in profound uncertainty. The reasonable answers you have heard often conflict and leave you still wondering. But philosophy, as Socrates and Aristotle suggest [see Plato, *Theaetetus*, 155; Aristotle, *Metaphysics*, Bk. I, ch. 2, 982ᵇ], begins with wonder.

   It is worth pursuing these questions methodically and with persistence. You will find some valuable answers worked out by philosophers, and you will be invited to evaluate their accomplishments as well as to think out new solutions. The celebrated answers include God as Creator (Augustine), atoms and void as the origin and substance of the universe (Democritus), matter and mind as the dual reality of things including our body and soul (Descartes), and real things as nothing more or less than ideas of the mind (Berkeley). The branch of philosophy concerned with first principles, the philosophy of reality, is known by the traditional title of *metaphysics*. It is a post-Aristotelian word, meaning after or beyond (*meta*) physics. Aristotle designated this field as "first philosophy," a name also used by some later thinkers. *Ontology* (from Gr.: *onta*, "being") is the branch of metaphysics that studies questions of being. *Cosmology* studies the origin and structure of the universe (Gr.: *kosmos*).

Epistemology. Questions about the nature and purpose of what exists naturally give rise to questions about how we know about such purposes and existence. How do we know anything? What is knowledge? Granted that we can be deceived in many ways, including faulty notions and faulty sensations, what is the best method to obtain reliable knowledge? What does knowledge rely upon that mere belief doesn't have? What is the relationship between sensation, perception, conception, memory, imagination, abstraction, and intuition? Is there any kind of knowledge that is absolutely certain?

You are surrounded by a world seeking, dealing in, and imparting knowledge, but you may not have given any thought to such questions *about* knowledge. "All men by nature desire to know," Aristotle tells us in the opening words of his *Metaphysics* (Bk. I, ch. 1, 980ª), and the philosopher naturally desires to know about knowledge itself. If knowledge, as Socrates would have it, is "the food of the soul" [Plato, *Protagoras*, 313], then philosophy is a feast of feasts. Now is a good time to explore those questions, since it may give you a keener appreciation of the kinds of knowledge you are encountering in your college courses. The philosophy of knowledge is traditionally called *epistemology* (from Gr.: *episteme*, "knowledge or science").

Philosophy of science. Of all the kinds of knowledge special honor today is accorded that which we call scientific. What makes the special reasoning of science? Is it proper to speak of science in general or should we rather recognize that the sciences, in the plural, are unique and independent of one another? You have heard much about scientific method and scientific theories. What are the proper components of scientific method and how does science make proper use of theories? What conception of nature is operative in the sciences that inform us of nature? What is the role of explanation and prediction?

The practicing scientist usually does not consider such questions; he just goes ahead and does his valuable work, which is science. But as philosophers we ask such questions in order to get a better understanding of what the work of science is. This field is the *philosophy of science* (from Lat.: *scientia*, "organized knowledge").

Philosophy of religion. One of the problems raised for metaphysics is the existence of God. This also becomes a problem in the *philosophy of religion*, which considers such matters as the significance and nature of faith, the relationship of man to God, and the role of religion in human experience. While a religious training may inculcate certain precepts, assist one's faith, and answer problems by reference to Holy Scripture, the philosophy of religion is a critical inquiry which applies intellectual standards to the understanding and assessment of such religious activities. Do not expect philosophy to offer what you have been offered in religion. *Theology* (from Gr.: *theos*, "god") may be thought of as a discipline distinct from philosophy in that it explores questions concerning God given a religious commitment of some kind. The School of Theology in the medieval university was separate from the philosophy faculty, and that generally is the case today in denominational institutions.

The branches so far sketched have in common a concern for the structure and operation of things. They probe what constitutes existence, knowledge, science, God. Philosophy also deals with the human subject and its experiences, aspirations, values, and fulfillment. The philosophy of religion does so insofar as it treats religion as a part of human experience. Epistemology can explore human subjectivity, the foundations of our understanding, and the relationship of values to factual knowledge. Other branches of philosophy treat values in man's actions, individually and collectively, and in man's imagination and aesthetic experience.

Ethics. *Ethics* is that branch of philosophy which explores the good life. The good life, or "happiness," is something we all want. Are you not attending college in order to make your life better? Or is the purpose of higher education to permit you to make a better living? What is the relationship between wealth and goodness? What do you want out of life? What does life have to offer you? Which is primary: health, love, fame, power, pleasure, knowledge, virtue? While you probe the intimate questions of what your life means to you and what you ought to do with your life, keep in mind that you live among others. The fulfillment of your happiness rests in part upon the existence of others, but the activities of others may also interfere with your happiness. What, then, are your responsibilities toward others? What may you expect and require of them? Ethics is a field of philosophy that has an appeal to all reflective men and women, because it inquires into how we should live and this is a problem no living man or woman can escape. The word "ethics" derives from the Greek: *ethos*, "character."

Substantive ethics deals with concrete problems to be resolved in life by the individual, e.g. "Should I become addicted to euphoric drugs?" *Descriptive ethics* analyzes established behavior and beliefs, e.g. "What are our operative principles concerning nonmarital sexual intercourse?" *Normative ethics* seeks to establish particular value judgments, e.g. "Ought we never to lie?" *Metaethics* inquires into the language and conceptual foundations of ethical theory, e.g. "What is the meaning and justification for any 'ought' claim?" *Social ethics* concentrates on responsibility to others and social policy, e.g. "Should pornography be censored?" An ethics course may mix these sub-branches in any proportion.

Political philosophy. Not only do humans interact as individuals in society; institutions have a character and a power of their own. The State is such an institution. It can be argued that the State is the framework which permits any other institution to be formed or people to act in certain ways. There are different kinds of States and governments. What are the advantages and hazards of each? What do we mean by such treasured notions as "democracy," "freedom," "rights"? What moral limits must be operative on political power? Does might make right? What principles should guide the conduct of States among one another in a world constantly threatened with destruction by war? These are questions for *political philosophy*, which explores the nature of political organization.

Social philosophy. Political philosophy may join hands with social ethics in a fresh study of the organization and values of *society*, of which government might be but one institution. This is *social philosophy*, which is emerging as a distinct field concerned with the nature of social life and institutions. It delves into such problems as racism, poverty, ecology, privacy, and sexual morality.

Aesthetics. Human values involve not only what is good and right but also what is enjoyable and creative. What is beauty? What is art? What standards of judgment can there be for distinguishing good art or genuine beauty? Is each person's taste as good as another's? What good is taste to a person? What is the value of artistic creation and of aesthetic experience in human life? Questions of this kind are addressed by the branch of philosophy known as *aesthetics*, or the philosophy of art and beauty. The name is from the Greek *aisthesis*, meaning "sensation," and was assigned to this field in the eighteenth century by Baumgarten.

Aesthetics is concerned with three large areas: (1) the nature of *art;* (2) the nature of artistic *creation;* and (3) the nature of aesthetic *experience* whether it be of works of art or of perceptions and activities. In addition to the beautiful, aesthetics may study the tragic, comic, grotesque, and ugly.

Value theory. Values are something we cannot live without. Every day we make value judgments about things and activities. Man is pre-eminently a value-being, inescapably engaged in seeking, finding, positing, judging, creating, or enjoying values.

What then are values? What is their relationship to facts? How do the different kinds of values (such as aesthetic, religious, moral) function? How are they related? What are we to do with the variety of conflicting values in any one area of human concern? What kinds of arguments are available for and against any proposed set of values? What is of highest value? These questions are at the heart of a special branch of philosophy called *value theory* or, more technically, *axiology* (from Gr.: *axios,* "worth").

Logic. All of the branches of philosophy mentioned are distinguishable by the problematic areas they deal with. In each area they examine arguments, construct arguments, work on proofs, and test theories. But you may ask, "What constitutes a proper argument or a valid proof? What are the criteria for judgment?" The branch of philosophy dedicated to the art or science of argument is called *logic.* This is a late Greek name for the field, derived from the versatile word *logos,* meaning reason, speech, statement, argument, or discussion. The earlier name was *organon* (Gr.: "instrument"). Logic is also known as the art of making inferences and the art of correct thinking.

There are, interestingly, alternatives for the positing of logical rules and procedures within any branch of logic. This gives a certain freedom to logic. But there is also a need to adopt some conventions as to what procedures to follow for the sake of argument. Once adopted these are to be applied strictly. This gives logic its rigor. Currently taught are two schools of *deductive logic* in which claims can be derived from prior general claims. (1) The traditional Aristotelian or Scholastic Logic employs certain formal arrangements of statements called syllogisms, which are expressed in a natural language, e.g. English. (2) Modern Symbolic Logic, closely allied with the foundations of mathematics, represents arguments by means of combinations of symbols.

The introductory logic course will probably include some work in *induction*, by which general claims are grounded on the evidence of particular instances, as well as *informal logic*, which deals with ambiguities, fallacies, definition, and other problems in language. *Dialectical logic* is an important instrument for resolving conflicts in claims and expanding understanding, but it is rarely taught in American schools. (For more on deduction and induction see ch. 4 and consult these terms in the Glossary, ch. 5.)

Logic is operative in all the branches of philosophy and every field of knowledge. To John of Salisbury it is the very soul of philosophy. [John of Salisbury, *The Metalogicon*, trans. Daniel D. McGarry (Berkeley, Cal.: University of California Press, 1962), Bk. II, ch. 6, p. 84.] A separate course in logic is likely to be available at your school in addition to the general introduction to philosophy. In this way a full term can be devoted to developing skills in careful examination of argument.

History of philosophy.   Division of philosophy into branches dealing with problems in distinct areas may create strange bedfellows, for it throws together authors of different centuries and cultures. Such an assemblage of minds helps us to see the problems in their fullness. It is also desirable to see the thought of a particular thinker in its fullness and within the intellectual context of his time and working place. Sometimes it is important, as in the case of Plato, to see the connections between all of a philosopher's work in what we have taken the liberty of separating into branches. An author generally responds to other thinkers, his predecessors and contemporaries, and other thinkers respond in turn to that author.

The *history of philosophy* is that branch of philosophy which examines philosophical work in all branches within the contexts of a thinker's traditions and background. Sometimes the beginning course in philosophy will be a survey of the history of philosophy rather than a selection of branches. American colleges may be counted upon to have at least one course available in the history of philosophy and sometimes an entire sequence tracing major epochs, including Ancient, Medieval, Modern (generally from the seventeenth to the nineteenth century), and Recent or Contemporary.

History of ideas.   *History of ideas* studies the changes in a major idea, such as justice, nature, freedom, over time. It is a valuable way of connecting varied conceptions of a common problem. History of ideas can have a place in many other disciplines besides philosophy as the analysis of the development of their key concepts. In philosophy a course in history of ideas will bear the title of the particular idea to be studied.

Oriental philosophy. Special mention must be made of *Oriental philosophy*, which is becoming increasingly available as a college course in America. This is not a branch of philosophic problems, strictly speaking, nor does it constitute a distinct stage in the worldwide history of philosophy. Roughly speaking, it constitutes everything left out of Western philosophy—that is, most of the world of thought. Subdivisions include Indian, Chinese, Japanese, Islamic, and Buddhist philosophy. Every student in the Western Hemisphere would benefit from a course in non-Western studies as part of his general education. A philosophy course in this field will prove a mind-opener. It should help broaden your horizons not only in philosophy but in religion, art, and general culture.

There are three strong philosophic reasons for working in Oriental philosophy: (1) Such work has philosophic value though it is not the accustomed way of working in the West. It is an intellectual adventure in discovering other modes of thought.

(2) Such work equips one to look back, from the different perspectives of the East, upon the traditional problems and distinctions of Western philosophy. There is the possibility of another intellectual adventure, that of seeing our problems from the standpoints of other modes of thought.

(3) In addition, such work can lead to insights concerning the great questions of philosophy about life, meaning, and existence. You might learn that there are questions that are not particularly Eastern or Western but universal. Oriental philosophy might show you that Oriental modes of thought are not foreign to you, so that you need not remain a mere Westerner. This is philosophy's grandest adventure of all, in which you discover your humanity.

Other branches. There are many other branches in philosophy. We only have space for naming some and mentioning a few of their notable problems.

Philosophy of history (a name given the field in the eighteenth century): Are there laws of history? Does the march of history have a purpose or destination? What place does human freedom have in history? What are proper historical method and explanation?

Philosophy of law or *legal philosophy:* What is the relationship between law and morality? What is the relationship between legal systems and political order? What are the justifications and the limits of
law?

Philosophy of culture: Are all cultural values relative? What are the
cultural preconditions to ethical conduct and philosophical discourse?
What role does religion, art, or philosophy play in a culture?

Philosophy of language: Is there a universal grammar to fit all languages? Does language have inherent logical structure? What do we
mean when we say something? What do we say when we mean something?

Philosophy of the social sciences: How do the social sciences rate as
science? What are the methods, presuppositions, and structures of an-
thropology, sociology, psychology?

It should be clear that a "philosophy of" course may be offered in
virtually any intellectual field.

Passages for study

1. . . . . there are no particular philosophical sciences, standing by
themselves. Philosophy is unity, and when we treat of Æsthetic or of
Logic or of Ethics, we treat always of the whole of philosophy, although illustrating for didactic purposes only one side of that insepa-
rable unity. [Benedetto Croce, *Æsthetic as Science of Expression and General Linguistic*, trans. Douglas Ainslie (New York: Noonday Press,
1955), Preface, pp. xxvii–xxviii.]

2. In our own age everything is mixed up together: the aesthetic is
treated ethically, faith is dealt with intellectually, and so forth. Philosophy has answered every question; but no adequate consideration
has been given the question concerning what sphere it is within which
each question finds its answer. This creates a greater confusion in the
world of the spirit than when in the civic life an ecclesiastical question, let us say, is handled by the bridge commission. [Søren Kierkegaard, *Concluding Unscientific Postscript*, trans. David F. Swenson and
Walter Lowrie (Princeton, N.J.: Princeton University Press, "Princeton Paperback," 1968), p. 288.]

3. The relation between æsthetic and moral judgments, between
the spheres of the beautiful and the good, is close, but the distinction
between them is important. One factor of this distinction is that while
æsthetic judgments are mainly positive, that is, perceptions of good,
moral judgments are mainly and fundamentally negative, or perceptions of evil. Another factor of the distinction is that whereas, in the

perception of beauty, our judgment is necessarily intrinsic and based on the character of the immediate experience, and never consciously on the idea of an eventual utility in the object, judgments about moral worth, on the contrary, are always based, when they are positive, upon the consciousness of benefits probably involved. [George Santayana, *The Sense of Beauty* (New York: Dover, 1955), Pt. I, §3, p. 23.]

4. One cannot escape ontology if one wants to know! For knowing means recognizing something as being. And being is an infinitely involved texture, to be described by the never-ending task of ontology. [Paul Tillich, *Love, Power, and Justice: Ontological Analyses and Ethical Applications* (London: Oxford University Press, "A Galaxy Book," 1971), p. 20.]

5. Just as we attempt to formulate in precise terms our sense experience in the natural sciences, even so philosophy of religion attempts to define the world to which our religious experiences refer. [Sarvepalli Radhakrishnan, *An Idealist View of Life* (London: George Allen & Unwin, 2nd ed., 1957), p. 85.]

Bibliography

1. Metaphysics
Ayer, A. J. *Metaphysics and Common Sense* (San Francisco: Freeman, Cooper & Company, 1970).
De George, Richard T. (ed.). *Classical and Contemporary Metaphysics* (New York: Holt, Rinehart and Winston, 1962).

2. Epistemology
Ackermann, Robert J. *Theories of Knowledge: A Critical Introduction* (New York: McGraw-Hill, 1965).
Arner, Douglas C. *Perception, Reason, and Knowledge: An Introduction to Epistemology* (Glenview, Ill.: Scott, Foresman, 1972).

3. Philosophy of Science
Hanson, Norwood Russell. *Perception and Discovery: An Introduction to Scientific Inquiry* (San Francisco: Freeman, Cooper & Company, 1969).
Humphreys, Willard C. *Anomalies and Scientific Theories* (San Francisco: Freeman, Cooper & Company, 1968).

4. Philosophy of Religion
Diamond, Malcolm L. *Contemporary Philosophy and Religious Thought: An Introduction to the Philosophy of Religion* (New York: McGraw-Hill, 1974).
Ross, James F. *Introduction to the Philosophy of Religion* (New York: Macmillan, 1969).

5. Ethics

Johnson, Oliver A. (ed.). *Ethics: Selections from Classical and Contemporary Writers* (New York: Holt, Rinehart and Winston, 3rd ed., 1974).

Ross, Stephen David. *In Pursuit of Moral Value* (San Francisco: Freeman, Cooper & Company, 1974).

———. *Moral Decision: An Introduction to Ethics* (San Francisco: Freeman, Cooper & Company, 1972).

6. Political and Social Philosophy

Brandt, Richard B. (ed.). *Social Justice* (Englewood Cliffs, N.J.: Prentice-Hall, "A Spectrum Book," 1962).

Downton, James V., and Hart, David K. (eds.). *Perspectives on Political Philosophy*, 2 vol. (New York: Holt, Rinehart and Winston, 1971).

7. Aesthetics

Rader, Melvin (ed.). *A Modern Book of Esthetics: An Anthology* (New York: Holt, Rinehart and Winston, 4th ed., 1973).

Steinkraus, Warren E. *Philosophy of Art* (Beverly Hills, Cal.: Benziger, 1974).

8. Value Theory

Dewey, John. *Theory of Valuation*, Vol. II, No. 4 of the *International Encyclopedia of Unified Science* (Chicago: University of Chicago Press, 1939).

Frondizi, Risieri. *What Is Value? An Introduction to Axiology*, trans. Solomon Lipp (LaSalle, Ill.: Open Court, "Open Court Classics," 2nd ed., 1971).

9. Logic

Copi, Irving M. *Introduction to Logic* (New York: Macmillan, 4th ed., 1972).

Kneale, William and Martha. *The Development of Logic* (Oxford: Clarendon Press, 1962).

10. History of Philosophy

Hampshire, Stuart (ed.). *The Age of Reason: The 17th Century Philosophers* (New York: New American Library, "Mentor Book," 1956).

Nahm, Milton C. *Selections from Early Greek Philosophy* (New York: Appleton-Century-Crofts, 4th ed., 1964).

Shapiro, Herman (ed.). *Medieval Philosophy* (New York: Modern Library, 1964).

White, Morton (ed.). *The Age of Analysis: 20th Century Philosophers* (New York: New American Library, "Mentor Book," 1955).

Note: See listings of histories of philosophy under reference works, ch. 8.

11. History of Ideas

Donner, Morton; Eble, Kenneth E.; and Helbling, Robert E. (eds.). *The Intellectual Tradition of the West: Readings in the History of Ideas,* 2 vol. (Glenview, Ill.: Scott, Foresman, 1967–1968).

Lovejoy, Arthur O. *Essays in the History of Ideas* (New York: Putnam's, "Capricorn Books," 1960).

12. Oriental Philosophy

Chan, Wing-tsit (ed.). *A Source Book in Chinese Philosophy* (Princeton, N.J.: Princeton University Press, 1969).

Müller, F. Max (ed.). *The Sacred Books of the East,* 51 vol. (Oxford: Clarendon Press, 1875–1897).

Radhakrishnan, Sarvepalli, and Moore, Charles A. (eds.). *A Source Book in Indian Philosophy* (Princeton, N.J.: Princeton University Press, 1957).

13. Other Branches

   A. Philosophy of History

Meyerhoff, Hans (ed.). *The Philosophy of History in Our Time* (Garden City, N.Y.: Doubleday, "Anchor Books," 1959).

   B. Philosophy of Law

Kent, Edward Allen (ed.). *Law and Philosophy: Readings in Legal Philosophy* (New York: Appleton-Century-Crofts, 1970).

   C. Philosophy of Culture

Verene, Donald Phillip (ed.). *Man and Culture: A Philosophical Anthology* (New York: Dell, 1970).

   D. Philosophy of Language

Rosenberg, Jay F., and Travis, Charles (eds.). *Readings in the Philosophy of Language* (Englewood Cliffs, N.J.: Prentice-Hall, 1971).

   E. Philosophy of the Social Sciences

Natanson, Maurice (ed.). *Philosophy of the Social Sciences: A Reader* (New York: Random House, 1963).

   F. Philosophy of Mathematics

Baum, Robert J. *Philosophy and Mathematics: From Plato to the Present* (San Francisco: Freeman, Cooper & Company, 1974).

3

How to Read Philosophy

Primary and secondary sources. Supposing, then, that your course will cover problems in one or more areas of philosophical work, we can look at the ways in which it will make use of readings to explore the problems.

Readings may be divided into primary and secondary sources. A *primary source* is a text that is studied for its own contribution. A *secondary source* is a work that is studied for the light it may throw on primary sources. Secondary sources may be informational, analytic, or critical. They include commentaries, introductions, scholarly articles, and reference materials. Most of the readings required for a beginning course in philosophy are likely to be primary materials. In this way you get to cut your teeth on the celebrated texts in the career of philosophy. You should try to master first-rate philosophical writing without becoming dependent upon secondary materials.

Sometimes a few secondary sources are assigned not only to help in your work on the basic texts but to illustrate important insights of later authors. Philosophy is a discipline where secondary sources may become primary, as what is intended as a discussion of another author may develop into a major original view of basic significance. Much philosophic writing in the Middle Ages took the form of commentaries on primary texts and even upon other commentaries.

You may be using a textbook which interprets primary sources but is intended as the primary material for your work in the course. Thus, you might not be expected to verify what it claims of Descartes or Hume but rather to assess the philosophical worth of the author's position, supposing the historical accounts to be accurate. But in another course what counts may be the original positions of Descartes and Hume, while the interpretive volume is intended only to be instrumental to your grasp of those positions. It is crucial that you clearly distinguish between primary and secondary materials and that you understand how and when to make use of each kind.

Format of textbooks. There is a variety of *reading formats* available for use in philosophy. Try to locate your textbooks among these types so that you will know what to expect from them and how to best make use of them. A text is something written, whether a sentence or a book. A textbook is a volume published for study in courses. Textbooks contain texts. The formats required in a philosophy course include: (1) a compilation of selections from primary sources grouped about problems or organized under the branches of philosophy; (2) a handful of separate, usually paperback, editions of full-length primary texts, some of which may present alternative views of sets of problems; (3) a textbook written by a single author as a primary or secondary volume, incorporating his presentation of a variety of opposing arguments in addition to the author's own views; (4) a textbook that presents the author's own arguments on the issues as a primary source. Whatever the format, you should keep your eye out for a number of ways of treating a problem, a group of problems in a field, or the constitutive issues in a problem.

Reader in philosophy. The *reader* may offer you half a dozen short selections on one or two key problems within each branch to be studied. The advantage in using such selections is that they are brief enough to be read and discussed in a short period, enabling a class to consider a number of alternatives in a few weeks. You can attack the issues from several sides. The reading selections represent possibilities in perspective and argument. Sometimes you will not see the value in a particular selection until after you have read others which round out the problem. As you study each selection, then, turn your mind to the problem that is under treatment.

Mastery of the readings will probably be your first task in beginning philosophy. This means you must think about the authors' thinking as well as what the authors are thinking about. Indeed, you can't master the readings as forms of thought without giving thought to the problems that are being considered.

Confusion may be the early fruit of philosophic reading as you discover authors at cross-purposes or with incommensurable procedures. One student expressed this in a course evaluation: "The readings were so contradictory that I could not get a foundation to form a basis to work from." But this confusion may be a sign that not enough serious attention has been given to the complexity and difficulty of the problems discussed. You may not have noticed them as genuinely problematic. Early confusion of this kind may also be a sign that you are encountering a surprising richness of philosophical argument, a diversity of methods, or an ingenuity of reasoning. Two or more readings on a problem may alert you to issues you have been missing and bring you to think about them. *The reading selections are instruments for bringing you around to grapple with the problems.* Use each instrument in turn to find out what it can do. Weigh the merits of the several views in comparison with one another. Be prepared to work out new alternatives, hopefully sounder ones, that ought to apply to the problem under discussion.

No reading should be undertaken in an intellectual vacuum. Think of other appropriate possibilities. This is not a game of inventing alternatives. Our goal is to find the best answer.

In sum, your responsibilities as a reader of philosophy are: understand each selection on its own terms; compare and weigh the several pertinent selections as contributions to the same subject; find and defend the best resolution of the problem, whether it is in the readings or not.

There are disadvantages to exploring problems by the use of readings in compilation. For one thing, you depend on the editor's skill at selecting parts of longer works by several authors and juxtaposing them. You may find as you closely follow an author's argument that part of it has been excised by the editor because of limitations of space. Do not let the editor's taste or the exigencies of textbook publishing keep you from following the rest of the argument. Go to the library and consult the complete text.

A book may be as useful working from the back as from the front cover if you know what you are looking for. Look at what else besides readings your textbook reader may have in store for you if you should need it. See if it has a glossary, index, general introduction, explanatory introductions, biographical notes, footnotes, illustrations, and bibliographies.

Separate editions. Philosophy instructors often find it desirable to use longer works, available in inexpensive editions, so that more time can be spent tracing out the author's full-length position on a great problem or in a distinct field. It takes much longer this way to get the position clearly exposed and amply discussed, but the several class meetings devoted to the one author will be rewarding in depth. Fewer authors can be included in a course employing this format than by using a reader.

It may seem at first that the authors of the *separate editions* are not talking about the same issues. You do not have the help of an editor who has put related material together and trimmed away tangential arguments. Therefore, you, with the help of the instructor, will have to do the job of relating the texts, pinpointing their common problems, and leaving aside extraneous discussions.

Unified presentation. Authors do not always give a fair representation of the arguments of their opponents; they might not even mention the views of others when they offer their own insights. When separate editions are used or selections from a compilation, the philosophers might not appear to be joining issue. Each argument seems to be offered with little attention to the other pertinent arguments. A way to overcome these disadvantages is to use a *textbook written entirely by one philosopher* who tries to represent fairly the major opposed positions on fundamental problems. The confrontations are arranged by the author, who may take a hand in their evaluation and resolution. The varieties of style in which arguments have been couched by men and women at different periods and in different languages will no longer distract the reader, for you are offered a *uniform exposition* written in English by a contemporary philosopher. A work of this kind can rapidly open up a broad field of work for you to scan.

The disadvantages should be evident. The one thinker whose book you read must bear on his shoulders the weight of all the arguments in the course. Undoubtedly, such an author could be helped out at points by a Plato, Aristotle, Kant, or Hegel, speaking for themselves. It would be unusual for one philosopher to grasp with equal insight and to represent with equal clarity the work of all great philosophers. But no matter how accurate and lucid the exposition of the arguments, you must still attempt to resolve the problems. Though the author of the uniform presentation may attempt to resolve them for you, you will have to confront the question as to whether his are the right answers.

Sometimes there are more insights to be had in working with opposed one-sided works than with a work that treats opposed ideas equally and fairly. Yet a uniform presentation helps you get into the problems with greater ease by clarifying the contending sides. If you have some doubts about the sense of a philosopher explicated by your uniform textbook, or else a special interest in the ideas attributed to that philosopher, do some reading in the primary texts in the library.

Primary textbook. There are also *textbooks written as primary sources* to make available the views of the author for discussion. References to other philosophers are made to support the author's position or for historical reasons. If the author considers opposed arguments on certain issues it is to show us which he thinks are the best arguments.

The convenience of this format is that you have both a uniform presentation of problems and a primary text by one author. Ease and intensity of study are thus both possible. The danger of such a textbook is that you will passively accept what you read as you may have been accustomed to by secondary school. Or you may use your philosophy book as if it were the factual authority in the same sense as your textbook in biology or your general volume in history. All you might get out of the course is an uncritical acquaintanceship with the philosophy of a particular textbook writer rather than an initiation into philosophical activity.

Even when such a book is required there is an obligation for you to seek out a plurality of views on the subjects treated. The instructor and the class will call for arguments in contrast with those of the author. You will have to evaluate the author's arguments to show awareness of alternative approaches to the problems. Though the textbook seems to solve everything, the coursework may unsolve it all. Textbooks are not identical with courses. No one book makes all of philosophy.

An exercise in reading.   Francis Bacon, in the section "The New Organon" of his work *The Great Instauration*, presents a series of "Aphorisms concerning the Interpretation of Nature and the Kingdom of Man," the first of which reads:

> Man, being the servant and interpreter of Nature, can do and understand so much and so much only as he has observed in fact or in thought of the course of nature; beyond this he neither knows anything nor can do anything. [Francis Bacon, *Works*, eds. James Spedding, Robert Leslie Ellis, and Douglas Denon Heath (New York: Hurd and Houghton), Vol. VIII (1869), Bk. I, No. i, p. 67.]

What is Bacon talking about? Man. What else? Nature. Specifically the relationship between man and nature. How is that relationship characterized? Man is both "servant" and "interpreter" of nature.

Please explain. A servant is one who is dependent upon a master. In what ways is man dependent upon nature? Both his "doing" and his "understanding" are limited, according to Bacon, by what he has "observed" concerning nature. Notice that if man's understanding is dependent upon what he knows of nature, then he will have certain limitations as "interpreter" of nature.

If "understanding" and "interpreting" are two words for the same thought, then "doing" and "serving" may be equivalent. The closing words of the aphorism indicate that Bacon's dual subject is knowledge and action. Thus, the word "servant" must be understood in a broader sense than mere subservience or dependency.

The word "observed" also has to be carefully understood in the context of the statement, for Bacon speaks of observing nature in thought. How does one do that? What is the connection, if any, between direct observation of nature "in fact" and this curious observation "in thought"? We look forward to Bacon's clarification of this point; we will have to be observant as we follow his reasoning.

Here is his second aphorism:

> Neither the naked hand nor the understanding left to itself can effect much. It is by instruments and helps that the work is done, which are as much wanted for the understanding as for the hand. And as the instruments of the hand either give motion or guide it, so the instruments of the mind supply either suggestions for the understanding or cautions.

Bacon continues to discuss the two human functions of doing and knowing. Here he is concerned with the natural shortcomings of such functions. It is obvious that by means of tools we can overcome some of the physical shortcomings and increase the power of our hands. Constructing an analogy, Bacon argues that there are also appropriate "instruments" for the mind to help it accomplish its work. He differentiates two kinds of these instruments: those that give suggestions and those that supply cautions. Or, to put it entirely in our own words: Man's understanding can be assisted in its tasks by intellectual methods which indicate how he ought to proceed as well as what he ought to avoid in his thinking.

The discussion of mental instruments throws light on the purpose of the work indicated in the title "New Organon." I'm sure you have discovered the meaning of "organon" (by using a dictionary or even this handbook) as instrument. Bacon, then, appears to be setting forth a new program for the mind's implementation. Perhaps the method that can be outlined for the understanding will bring about the "Great Instauration" mentioned in the main title of Bacon's work. I am sure you will find out what *that* means. By the way, if Bacon is proposing a new organon, what is wrong with the old one? We would have to look for his discussion of this as we read further.

But let's not push on too quickly with our reading, for we might skip over points requiring examination. Isn't there a mistake in spelling in the words "can effect much"? Doesn't Bacon mean "can affect much"? What *is* the difference between these two phrases? Just what is the point that Bacon is driving at? Put it in your own words.

Bacon's third aphorism is:

> Human knowledge and human power meet in one; for where the cause is not known the effect cannot be produced. Nature to be commanded must be obeyed; and that which in contemplation is as the cause is in operation as the rule.

Here he draws the connection between knowing and doing. In order to do something, Bacon suggests, we have to operate on its appropriate causes. But the identification of the correct cause for any effect is a question of knowledge. It follows that the more we know about causes, or "the course of nature," the more we will be able to do things in the world, or command nature. In brief, knowledge is power. Action is guided by rules just as understanding ("contemplation") is guided by causes. What serves as cause can also serve as rule. Notice how we have had to reword in a positive sense what is implied by the negative wording of the text: "for where the cause is not known the effect cannot be produced."

Texts lead somewhere.   We will not read further in Bacon's text (there are 179 more aphorisms), although you should feel the need to do so in order to make fuller sense of the few lines we have read together. This exemplifies an important feature of philosophical reading: *a text in philosophy leads somewhere.* We have to follow it if we are to judge the value of its beginning claims. Clarification of many points along the way must wait until other points are raised. But as we read on we find new points being introduced calling for further clarification. Thus, while reading we are obliged to look forward and backward in thought. We try to piece each passage in the text into the context of the author's unfolding reasoning. We try to get through the words to the reasoning; *we have to read the mind of the text.*

Re-reading.   *This means that more than one reading is needed.* A first reading might be the line-by-line disentanglement of the meaning of the statements, of a kind we have started on Bacon. A second reading might shift from the trees to the forest, i.e., to an examination of the argument as a whole as it runs through the text. This kind of reading you can now do in reading again the three aphorisms we have explicated.

It is rather difficult at the beginning to do both kinds of reading at once. Thus, a third reading may match up the sense of the whole with the language of the lines, double-checking what you have found as the reasoning. A fourth reading is advisable at some later date, say after the text has been discussed in class or after you have acquired some insights on the same problem from reading other selections, such as Descartes. You will be amazed by the new light in which you see an essay after a space of only a few weeks' reflection on related problems. The fourth reading is also useful in reviewing the coursework for examinations.

Some texts you may *have* to read additional times during the course. Do not set yourself a limit. Keep re-reading until you are satisfied that you understand the work. Of course, you might not be satisfied with any of your readings of a text during a course. Do the best you can with the time available. Do not read the text in order to memorize it; approach it each time with resharpened tools of analysis and evaluation. Some works in philosophy like some works in literature prove continually rewarding over a lifetime of re-reading.

Guidelines. Our brief reading in Bacon exemplifies some of the pertinent things we can do with a text. Here are some *guidelines for reading philosophy:*

(1) We must maintain a tolerance toward the author. Give the author a chance to say what he has to say in his own words. Recognize that he can't say everything at once. It takes time to explain points, to make distinctions, and to arrive at consequences. We must be patient and attentive if we are to understand what he has to say.

(2) We must be prepared to accept a certain flexibility of language in what the author says. This is especially true when reading a translation or a work written in another century. The selections from Bacon that we studied were composed in Latin and were rendered into English by his editors in the seventeenth century. Words may be used in the text in special senses which are not the ordinary ways you would use them. Be sure to see how such words are actually *used,* for their use in context will show you the meaning given them by the author.

(3) We have to keep asking ourselves what the author is talking about. What is his subject? What is at issue? Try to get through the words to the problem. You can't afford to be so tied up with the particular words used that you miss the ideas which could have been presented in other words.

(4) Be awake to the distinctions drawn. Take note of how the author divides the subject, distinguishes the issues, identifies the scope or method of the discussion, and defines the key concepts.

(5) Look for the principles. These are the argumentative starting points, the commitments, axioms, assumptions, definitions, hypotheses from which the reasoning proceeds. Ask yourself, "What is it all based upon?"

(6) Trace the movement of the inquiry and argument. See in what directions the reasoning moves and what steps it takes. At each point ask, "How did the author get to this point from the preceding points? Where can the author get from this point?" Analyze the kinds of argument present and their use of fact, common beliefs, assumptions, probabilities, certainties, analogies, etc.

(7) Check the author's conclusions against his principles and arguments. Identify the reasoning and evidence employed by the author for each conclusion, even if some supporting features are unspoken. Don't concentrate exclusively on isolating the author's conclusions, or "answers," but expose how the conclusions are arrived at, or the process of answering.

(8) Rephrase the reasoning in your own words. Break away from the style, the wording, the examples, and the presentational order of the text. Be ready to state your author's case in the clearest fashion employing plain but correct twentieth-century English, even if the author is utterly mistaken.

You will find extended treatment of the analysis of distinctions, principles, argument, and conclusions in philosophy in ch. 4.

Critical evaluation.   All this constitutes the first level of reading: understanding. But as you read you should also engage in another level: *critical evaluation*. At this level we ask:

Has the author made it clear what the problem is that he is working on?

Do the distinctions he makes help in treating that problem?

Does the language he uses bear ambiguities, inconsistencies, or a host of undefined terms?

Do his principles appear reasonable?

Are they worth our commitment?

What would happen to the author's position if we substituted other reasonable principles?

Does he argue with validity?

Is anything wrong with any of the arguments?

Are there objections to be made to the facts or evidence introduced?

What could be said in defense of the author's position that would rebut any of your criticisms?

In sum, what you seek to determine in your critical reading of the text is whether the author is right or wrong.

But a word of caution: *rarely will you find an entire text to be "right" or "wrong": usually you will find it right in some ways and wrong in others.* Your job in evaluation is to ascertain *precisely* what is right and what is wrong. Be on your guard against discarding faulty contributions that can be redeemed by certain corrections. Also be wary of swallowing the whole of some philosopher's line along with its hook and sinker. What matters in reading, say, Aquinas is not the grade you will give to Aquinas for being right or wrong but the assistance Aquinas will give you in grasping certain truths. It is necessary for you to develop fine philosophical discrimination whereby you can pinpoint valuable arguments and insights as well as faults and new difficulties.

When you first read philosophy you may think the author has done all the work and you merely have to gather the results from the page. It should soon become clear that it is you who have to do most of the work, including thinking for the author. Not only are you responsible for getting the author's thoughts out into the open, you are also responsible for getting your own thoughts out as you join issue with the author. You haven't *read* a work of philosophy unless you have joined issue. Joining issue means getting in there to struggle with the problem. Don't stand on the sidelines waiting: truths may pass you by or may not arrive. Pursue them. (For further discussion of critical evaluation see ch. 4 on reasoning and ch. 6 on writing.)

Reading as thinking. In concluding that an author is mistaken or confused in his reasoning, you are obliged to show exactly where and how he is mistaken and just what it is in the text that is confusing. On the other hand, if you find an author treats a problem successfully, you are obliged to show that he properly does so. *The burden of demonstration is upon you the reader.* No judgments are admissible unless fully supported by your reasons. Thus, the skill of reading philosophy requires the exercise of philosophical thinking, for what we have discussed as reading has been a kind of thinking. *Philosophical reading means an active engagement of the alert intellect with the reasoning set forth.* It involves questioning the text, sifting it, weighing it, reformulating it, *thinking it.* This is hard work but it is required in philosophy as well as all other intellectual disciplines. Few people read in such a way. You may be accustomed to reading passively, sweeping your eyes across the page, absorbing the words of the author and sometimes the information. *Thinking cannot be absorbed by such reading; thinking has to be thought.* A course in philosophy is an excellent occasion for you to learn how to read by using your head.

Marking the text. A practical suggestion to help your reading: *mark up your textbook.* As you read have a pencil and notepaper at hand. Underline or circle key statements or terms in the text. Marginal notations can be used to indicate the points of each paragraph. Numbering distinctions or reasons often helps to keep straight the reasoning over the course of an essay. Where there is a point or a term that gives you trouble put a question mark next to it so that you can return to it on second reading. All these writing acts are intended to aid your activity of analysis rather than to reduce the text for the sake of memorization. By putting questions or reformulations next to the text you place yourself in discussion with the work. If marking the text is to be of assistance, you must be selective. A student once showed me her copy of Kant in which every line of text had been underlined. She explained, "Everything he says seemed to me important."

You may wish to reformulate parts of the argument in your notebook as you read, or else write out in full your questions on the reading. Where a text is quite long, it is advantageous to outline its argument in your notebook with page references.

Words and allusions. You are responsible for making sense out of *every word and printed mark* in your assigned reading. If unfamiliar names, places, and events are referred to, look them up in a reference work. If you encounter new words, troublesome technical terms, or strange uses of old words, look them up in a dictionary. But remember, the dictionary only gives general account of how words have been used; it won't tell you what you want to know, namely the precise meaning of the words in your author's text. *You* will still have to determine that by close reading of his use of words in the context of his writing (on dictionaries see ch. 5 and ch. 8). Do your best to see that no obscurities remain in the text. If any do despite your efforts, mark them to be brought up in class.

Keep your eye out for possible printing errors. In one textbook I used, a printer's devil apparently had swallowed a line of Aquinas' proof of God's existence.

In identifying the allusions in a text you should also give some thought to their function in the text. Thus, a reading assignment had mentioned Plato's political advice concerning Syracuse, and the instructor called upon a student to locate Syracuse. The answer given was "Upstate New York."

Philosophy in translation. Many of the primary texts you read in philosophy are translations from other languages. A translation is a step beyond the primary, for it requires both an understanding of the original text and an interpretation of its meaning in your own language. Yet the translator may not fully understand what he is translating, and the translation may not fully communicate what he understands. The Italian proverb warns, *Traduttore, traditore,* whose exact translation is "Translator: traitor."

Keep in mind that there is more than one way to correctly translate a passage since languages do not have exact equivalences of meaning in structure or in words. A literal translation sticks close to the letter, matching word for word as much as possible. A translation of the spirit of the text tries to express the gist of the thinking in the clearest idiom of the second language. A too literal translation buries itself in the words to the detriment of the sense. A too liberal translation interprets the sense in a broad way that doesn't fit the words. A perfect translation would fit both the words and the sense of the original in exactly comparable garb of the second language. There are no perfect translations.

Like most prose, philosophy is translatable. That is, though there is a margin for missing the exact sense of the original text at any word, yet the reasoning may be so adequately captured in translation that we may work on it philosophically. Some key terms are often left in the original because of the lack of an English term; some of these terms have remained as words in our language. Examples are *Angst* and *Geist* from German, *hubris* and *catharsis* from Greek, *Karma* and *Nirvana* from Sanskrit. Words like these which spring from the world's tongues enrich the vocabulary of any one language as it speaks philosophically. Such words may be annotated in your textbooks, discussed in class, or looked up in philosophical and general dictionaries. Philosophers until recent years have had a fondness for quoting passages in other languages and ornamenting their texts with foreign terms. Thus, you may have to look up foreign words even in reading English texts. (On the use of technical terms in philosophy see ch. 5.)

Using other languages. If you have trouble following a passage in translation, it is helpful to consult other translations of the text. You might well try this with the passages from Bacon we studied. And it should be decisive to consult the original language of the work. The requirement of training in a language other than English has not completely disappeared from American colleges, so it may well be that you are studying such a language or have done so. Philosophy is a good course in which to make use of your language training. By looking up those troublesome passages or those great statements of truth when you are armed with the tools of language, you can clear up matters and get a firmer grasp on what is important.

After reading.   You are already thinking philosophically as you complete your philosophical reading. You have grasped the reasoning of the author and evaluated its correctness. But this thinking so far has been pursued in terms of the one author. Turn from consideration of the text to reflection upon the problem involved. See what the problem is, what its difficulties are, and what contribution the author makes toward resolving those difficulties.

Now think out the *other* difficulties that should be considered. What else is there to the problem left unexplored or unresolved by the author? What arguments could be presented in favor of conclusions opposed to those of the author? What other principles and other facts should be taken into account? How would you go about treating the problem? Where would you start? What evidence would you adduce? What reasoning would you follow?

See if you can construct clearly in your mind two or three distinct approaches to the problem, including the views of your author and yourself. Compare and contrast these views, set them into opposition, project their refutations of one another and their defenses in rebuttal. In short, *start a discussion going in your own mind.* Proper reading in philosophy inevitably leads to a dialogue. Feel free to put all your mental weight behind one position and then withdraw it in favor of another. Doubt your preferred views and give the benefit of the doubt to views you disfavor. There is a freedom here to make mistakes and to discover truth. It takes place in the volume of your mind. Close your printed book. Open your mind.

As you read various authors you will be enlarging the scope of your mental discussion. Minds like those of Plato, Aquinas, Kant will be joining yours. They will become participants in your own thought just as you participate in their thought when you read their works.

But reading philosophy means going beyond the readings to the philosophical issues at stake, no matter where they may lead. You must pursue what is only pointed to, and point to what is not proposed. In the midst of reading and considering proof of God's existence you might see a connection with the interesting problem of the existence of evil. That the latter is not assigned for consideration in the course or spelled out in the readings is no reason to resist speculating about it. Give yourself time and leisure and a quiet place to think. (On reading as part of your work for a term paper see ch. 6; on reading and re-reading for exams see ch. 7.)

Passages for study

1. Whoever therefore designs to read the following sheets, I entreat him that he would make my words the occasion of his own thinking, and endeavour to attain the same train of thoughts in reading that I had in writing them. By this means it will be easy for him to discover the truth or falsity of what I say. He will be out of all danger of being deceived by my words, and I do not see how he can be led into an error by considering his own naked, undisguised ideas. [George Berkeley, *A Treatise Concerning the Principles of Human Knowledge*, *Works*, Vol. I, ed. Alexander Campbell Fraser (Oxford: The Clarendon Press, 1871), Introduction, sec. 25, p. 154.]

2. I am a "skimmer" from way back—never reading a book sentence by sentence, word by word, rather glances at phrases here and there. In this course I was forced to read the subject matter very closely and look up words I didn't understand and stop and think about what each sentence meant. This helped me with my paper because I kept reading it over and over again to see if it was clear—what I was trying to get across. [Student comment.]

3. I didn't finish or digest any one text to my complete satisfaction and as such I have a "library" for future contemplations. [Student comment.]

4. Finally, if a lecturer or student encounters something very difficult to understand in Porphyry or any of the books, let him not be therewith deterred. Rather, let him go on, as authors mutually explain one another, and all things help in turn to explain other things. For which reason there is little or nothing that lies concealed from one who is well read. [John of Salisbury, *The Metalogicon*, trans. Daniel D. McGarry (Berkeley, Cal.: University of California Press, 1962), Bk. III, ch. 1, pp. 149–150.]

Bibliography

1. On reading

Adler, Mortimer J. *How to Read a Book: The Art of Getting a Liberal Education* (New York: Simon and Schuster, 1963).

Ross, Ralph; Berryman, John; and Tate, Allen. *The Arts of Reading* (New York: Thomas Y. Crowell, 1960), Pt. I, "Exposition and Argument."

2. General textbooks

Beck, Robert N. (ed.). *Perspectives in Philosophy: A Book of Readings* (New York: Holt, Rinehart and Winston, 1965).

Cornman, James W., and Lehrer, Keith. *Philosophical Problems and Arguments: An Introduction* (New York: Macmillan, 2nd ed., 1974).

Feinberg, Joel (ed.). *Reason and Responsibility: Readings in Some Basic Problems of Philosophy* (Encino, Cal.: Dickenson, 2nd ed., 1971).

Hospers, John. *An Introduction to Philosophical Analysis* (Englewood Cliffs, N.J.: Prentice-Hall, 2nd ed., 1967).

Note: Additional textbooks are listed under the several branches of philosophy in ch. 2.

3. Anthologies of primary sources

Burtt, Edwin A. (ed.). *The English Philosophers from Bacon to Mill* (New York: Modern Library, 1939).

McKeon, Richard (ed.). *Selections from Medieval Philosophers*, 2 vol. (New York: Scribner's, "Modern Student's Library," 1929–1930).

Oates, Whitney J. (ed.). *The Stoic and Epicurean Philosophers* (New York: Random House, 1940).

4. Classic works in philosophy available in various editions

Plato, *Republic*.

Aristotle, *Nicomachean Ethics*.

Augustine, *City of God*.

Plotinus, *Enneads*.

Aquinas, *Summa Theologica*.

Maimonides, *Guide for the Perplexed*.

Montaigne, *Essays*.

Descartes, *Meditations*.

Spinoza, *Ethics*.

Hobbes, *Leviathan*.

Locke, *Essay on Human Understanding*.

Newton, *Principia Naturalis*.

Vico, *The New Science*.

Hume, *Treatise of Human Nature*.

Kant, *Critique of Pure Reason*.

Hegel, *Phenomenology of Mind*.

Mill, *On Liberty*.

Marx, *Capital.*
Kierkegaard, *Either/Or.*
Schopenhauer, *The World as Will and Representation.*
Nietzsche, *Will to Power.*
James, *Pragmatism.*
Heidegger, *Being and Time.*

4

Reasoning Philosophically

In this chapter we discuss *the conduct of argument within philosophic thought*. First we will deal with the broad mental skills of argument: analysis, presupposition, evaluation, memory. Then we will take a brief look at the components or developments of argument that these skills apply to: definitions, principles, methods, forms of inference, ideas, theories, philosophies, and movements.

Argument.   Many of your important philosophic tasks involve argument. Argument is something you have been told to avoid in polite circles. Getting into an argument with your teachers is one of the taboos of secondary school. Argument, it seems, is not desirable in discussion because it disrupts cooperation. "To get into an argument is to get emotionally involved," explained one student at the beginning of a course in philosophy. "An argument is not rational," insisted another. A third beginner warned: "An argument is a verbal fight in which each side tries to beat the other by such things as emotional appeals, threats, and sometimes lies." But there is another sense of argument as the presentation of reasons. We may *argue for* a position on the grounds of appropriate supporting claims and evidence. We may *argue from* a position by developing the implications of its reasoning and applying it to fresh problems. We may *argue against* a position by criticizing its reasoning, challenging its supportive claims or evidence, and offering reasons for an opposed conclusion.

   Philosophy lives and breathes argument. One may argue that argument is the soul of philosophy. But one should also recognize that there is more substance to philosophy than argument alone; insight, intuition, doubt, and imagination have their place as well. In philosophy the class discussion will lead to argument. And philosophic arguments generally lead to discussion. The instructor will be arguing with you and you will be arguing with him. In philosophy there are *reasonable differences* concerning appropriate reasons, suitable evidence, proper objections, and correct procedure. As a consequence of this rich diversity in how we conceive the reasonable, much of our philosophical work is arguable—that is, subject to criticism as well as support. Thus, we spend much time analyzing arguments, constructing arguments, testing arguments, hunting for arguments, reformulating arguments, comparing arguments, and criticizing arguments. Philosophy is argumentative because it is fair and open discourse meant to demonstrate or discover the truth in debatable matters by the use of reason.

In such arguments disagreement is likely to appear. Disagreement in philosophy is not disagreeable. Indeed, it is often desirable. The phrase "I violently disagree" can never be appropriate in philosophy. But "I vigorously disagree" is permissible as long as you have strong reasons to offer.

Analysis. Your first responsibility when an argument is presented is to analyze it. Analysis is examination in depth—of arguments, positions, theories, concepts, terms, and problems. An analysis of an argument is the intellectual dissection of the discursive material that reveals the basic structure and important parts of the reasoning. An analysis is no simple descriptive report in which you represent the material in a brief fashion; it is an active engagement of your mind as it cuts through the material to the thinking within. The material presents the argument, but you must analyze it. To analyze is to investigate. You must go beneath the surface of words and the order of sentences in order to discover the argument.

Analysis is a habit of intellect that philosophy asks you to cultivate. Make this your duty: *any argument encountered is to be analyzed.* And you may add: *anything* presented philosophically is to be analyzed. Initially students have difficulties in getting down to analysis; you may be too subservient to the wording and sentence order of the material. Hence, you may find yourself preparing an outline, a paraphrase, a summary, a condensation of what is said, but these are only shorter presentations of the material rather than investigations of its reasoning and implications.

An analysis may be presented in language other than that of the text. Indeed, analysis *should* be presented in your own words. There is no need to restrict yourself to the style of the original when you are identifying the nature of its reasoning. However, it may be well to retain some key terms in order to show the chief distinctions in the argument. Once you discover the argument in the text or speech it exists in your mind and can be explained by you in your own words.

When you analyze an argument you examine which conclusions are arrived at concerning what issue by the use of what procedures starting from what foundations. Hence, there are four analytic questions you can ask about the argument: (1) What is the problem involved? (2) What is the answer to the problem? (3) How is that answer arrived at? (4) On what grounds does the answer stand? Your analysis may start at any one of these questions, and whichever one you start with should lead you to the others.

Examples. In analyzing an argument do not include the *examples* used unless there is a special reason to concentrate on them. Examples, strictly speaking, are not part of most arguments; they merely illustrate the arguments. Hence, the argument must stand on its own reasoning independently of its examples. If you understand an argument you can exemplify it. It is appropriate to analyze the original examples where the argument consists of nothing more than examples or where the examples used pose grave difficulties for the meaning or application of the argument, as, for example, in Kant's illustration of the categorical imperative in his *Foundations of the Metaphysics of Morals* (Sec. II). But poor examples are to be held against their author and not against the argument.

Absence of argument. You may discover in your efforts at analyzing an argument that *there is no argument.* There may be merely a set of claims without support or else a number of unconnected reasons. There may also be an enunciation of intuitions or of truths which are self-evident. When reference books or other authorities tell us the philosophy of so-and-so was such-and-such, what we are usually given are the conclusions reached by the thinker rather than the intellectual activity that leads to such conclusions. In such cases there is no argument presented for you to get your teeth into. A doctrine is a body of statements but an argument is a procedure of reasoning. In some cases you may find a position supported only by the plausibility of its consequences. The "argument" here is one of application, practice, or action.

Tacit argument. As you look for parts of the argument in the text or speech you may not find them all. That does not mean a deficiency in the work of the author or speaker. Many arguments in philosophy, and most arguments outside philosophy, have *unspoken parts* that are presumed to be understood by the audience. It is tedious to state everything. But the reasoning should make it clear enough just what the unspoken parts are. In your analysis of arguments you will frequently have to identify either tacit assumptions, presumed distinctions, operative definitions, or implicit conclusions. If you have to identify *all* these components in one case, there is no argument.

Facility in analysis. You will find, in your reading and in your reflections upon what is said in class, arguments that require extended study, but you will also have to make on the spot analyses in classroom and lecture hall. And you may alternate between construction and analysis of argument in your own thinking or writing. You should develop your skill to the point where you can analyze an argument in your sleep (in some classes, it seems, a few students do just that).

Presupposing the argument. Once you have grasped the argument your job is to see what contribution it makes. To do this you should be prepared to *presuppose or entertain the argument.* To presuppose an argument is to put it forth as an argument in your mind or in public even though you might not agree with it. You presuppose the argument for the sake of argument. It is not necessary that the argument entertain you; it is appropriate that you entertain it. By analyzing you identify the argument; by presupposing it you argue it out. To be fair to what the argument can do you have to put your mind into it, instead of just explaining the reasoning from the outside.

Presupposition does not mean a commitment to the argument and its conclusions. You may even find them reprehensible. But as a philosopher you must be willing to regard every argument as a potential path to the truth. To presuppose is to adopt hypothetically. You may well feel uneasy about arguing for things you reject, arguing by methods you disfavor, arguing from principles you do not share, but remember *it is only an argument.* See what it can do as you put your best efforts into it. In philosophy classes you will find yourself arguing about God, pleasure, democracy, and other topics you have strong feelings about. Be ready to entertain arguments on all sides of those questions no matter what your feelings or beliefs are. Philosophy requires a willing though temporary suspension of both belief and disbelief. It is a sign of maturity in philosophical discipline to be able to argue coherently and well for a position one does not accept.

In such cases credit is due not for making a bad case seem good but for making as good a case as legitimately can be made for a plausible approach to truth even if in the last analysis it doesn't succeed.

Plato was expert at putting the arguments of others in dialogue form and working with these animated views. In Scholastic Philosophy, the fair and full presentation of views one did not accept was built into the format of presenting one's arguments through a series of objections and replies (see, for example, Thomas Aquinas, *Summa Theologica*). Philosophers in modern times continue to use dialogue and the setting forth of objections by others to entertain arguments opposed to their own.

Responsibility as advocate. An argument that you have analyzed and not argued out is one that you don't take seriously. Arguing it out does not mean paraphrasing the original presentation. Once you have analyzed the structure of the meaning use your imagination to project the reasoning into the world of your own words. Imagination plays a large role in philosophy (more than is generally imagined). Imagination helps you to envision the way things could be, given certain arguments.

You now become responsible for the success of the argument of which you are the tentative advocate. This means you must do the best you can with it. Don't shortchange an argument because you disfavor it. Give it the strongest logical presentation you can muster. Improve the argument wherever possible while remaining true to its structure. An argument is not simply as good as its original author made it; it may be made better by another mind which remakes it. Philosophers carry on one another's work by re-arguing what has been argued before in one way or another. Though you initially find the argument in a text or in the thought of another, the real locus of any such argument is your mind.

It takes a while for you to become at home with the philosophic freedom of entertaining what is foreign to you. Once practiced in it you will find it enjoyable. You will be thinking things you never thought of, making a case for things you are against, and understanding what you do not believe. And others will be doing the same. Those who believe they have found the right answers and those who are at a loss can cooperate in the work upon arguments.

Assessing argument. It is not enough in philosophy to grasp every pertinent argument and to be prepared to argue it fairly. We would be deluged by a multitude of arguments though what we seek is the truth. What is necessary is *critical judgment. No argument you encounter or advance must pass unevaluated.* That is another of the intellectual responsibilities of the philosopher.

Judgment when exercised philosophically must be well founded, not capricious: "I don't like this argument." "It doesn't sound right." "This is great!" "Personally, I wouldn't argue this way." "I approve of this position." These are unacceptable as philosophical judgments; they are merely pronouncements of personal inclination. Judgment is not a reaction of feeling or habit, but a *reasoned assessment*. Hence, you have to arrive at your judgment by reasoning and you will have to give reasons for your judgment.

Oddly enough, the reasons for the judgment are more important to the work of the class than the outcome of the judgment. You may think of it in another light: *philosophic judgment is not a conclusion but a process of critical reasoning.* By following the reasons and testing them against the argument we will arrive at the final worth of the argument, but if you tell us the final worth without presenting your reasons we have nothing except your word for it. *Philosophy then becomes argument about argument.* As you might expect, there will be differing judgments of the same argument, so that your reasons must be subjected to close examination. Your assessment will be assessed.

Look for weaknesses in an argument. As you study it, analyze it, or present it, go through it with a fine-truth comb. Question and challenge it. In so doing you may find parts of the reasoning that do not stand up under the pressure. By probing for weaknesses you find them. But in so doing you will also find parts of the reasoning that stand up under the pressure. Subject them to renewed challenge. Be specific and exacting. Vagueness and rough judgment are worth little. Point out precisely what is wrong and explain why it is wrong. "Well, I think it is wrong," does not suffice.

Debating the merits. Judging the whole requires judging the parts, judging the parts requires judging the particulars of the argument. But be of two minds in this point-by-point assessment. With one mind do your best to demolish the argument at any point, with the other do your best to support it. You are responsible not only for *critically attacking* an argument that is open to criticism but also for *defending* it wherever possible against criticism. You are both prosecutor and defense attorney before the bar of reason. What comes under your critical scrutiny must include your critical scrutiny itself. Not only is the argument on trial but so is your mind for its fairness, pertinency, accuracy, consistency, and principled procedure. And to complete the courtroom metaphor, you have the additional responsibility of being the judge and jury in the case—that is, of determining whether the attack or the defense prevails upon each count.

Every argument no matter how sound can be criticized for not being some other argument which you prefer. That is superficial criticism. You must respect the argument for what it does accomplish, given its way of going about it. Suppose you were to hypothetically accept the premises of the argument, what good will that do in getting at the truth? Suppose for the sake of argument you were to accept the method; does it get us anywhere? Grant some of the key distinctions; see what results. What if the conclusions strike you as the right answers—have they been validly arrived at? Assessing argument obliges you to give and take. As you challenge one feature at a time hold in abeyance the rest of your challenges. See just what it takes for the argument to survive your successive challenges.

Criticism and evaluation. Philosophic understanding of argument occurs in analysis. Philosophic animation of argument occurs in presupposition. Philosophic appreciation of argument occurs in assessment. Philosophy is an art of criticism and evaluation. It is a perpetual faultfinder, problem-maker, and truth-seeker. But philosophic criticism ought not to be defeatist. If we work hard to smash arguments, shred ideas, and explode theories it is not out of hostility toward insight and reasoning; rather we are searching for what we can pick up of value from the pieces for the purposes of rebuilding.

Criticism is the double-checking of our constructions, it is preparatory to our inquiry, and it is revelatory of our values, for to be critical is to bring criteria to bear. In philosophy everything is open to criticism. Even philosophy. By "everything" we mean not the style nor the person but the reasoning.

It is easy to criticize but hard to be judicious. We must weigh our criticism to see how well it applies and how well it is answered so that we can judge the worth of the argument. This is critical evaluation. It is one of the most mature of intellectual skills. Good judgment, careful assessment, and balanced critical evaluation are different terms for much the same thing—something that requires ripening through intellectual experience and practice. This is what gets you answers in philosophy.

Relationship of skills. Analysis, presupposition, and evaluation of argument are *congenial skills.* To evaluate fairly you must understand; analysis and presupposition make that understanding available. An argument whose skeleton has once been laid bare by analysis begs to be given the flesh of presentation. An argument presented begs for assessment. The testing of an argument is a probing that opens it up to evaluation. Testing and evaluation throw new light on the parts and procedure of the argument so that the analysis may be completed or revised. Psychologically we probably engage in all three activities at once or in swift alternation, but philosophically we can separate and keep in order these accounts. Thus, you may be called upon at any moment to analyze an argument without arguing for it or assessing it, or to make the best possible case out of an argument without assessment, or to analyze and assess without arguing it.

Memory. Memory is the least distinguished of our higher mental powers, for it is mechanical and passive, not requiring our active understanding. To remember some bit of information is not necessarily to know it. Some people (whose names I have forgotten) are famous for their prestigious memories, but that doesn't make them well informed. Memory just as often preserves the dross and dust as the treasures. Augustine calls it the mere stomach of the mind. [Augustine, *The Confessions*, trans. Rex Warner (New York: New American Library, "A Mentor-Omega Book," 1963), Bk. X. ch. 15, p. 224.] Memory plays tricks upon us, and memory in all someday must fade or fail. But who truly understands will be able to understand once again when thinking upon the same matter. Train your memory and put it to its best use to help you. But do not build your intellectual life on it. Remember this: understanding may be what remains to the mind when all else is forgotten.

Definition. Would you like a definition of philosophical reasoning? Indeed, of philosophy itself? Yes! Fine, but what would you want in such a definition—that is, what should the definition contain and how would we determine it to be a fitting definition? That sounds like philosophy! It is. It is a philosophical question about definition. Ordinarily we pass over definitions quickly: it is assumed we know the definitions of what is spoken, and if we do not we can rapidly look them up. You may not have thought much about the purpose of definitions, their varieties, or their problems. Let us take a philosophic survey of *definitions* since they play various roles in philosophy.

There are many kinds of definition, for there are several purposes in defining things. We define in order to know what we are talking about, to bring clarity to the issues at stake, to move forward to the understanding of larger questions, to guide the direction of inquiry, and to expose the complexity of insights that comprises truth. Generally speaking, a definition sets limits: it marks the finitude (from the same Latin root: *finitus*) of something. In the Greek and Latin expressions definition is *a boundary marker*. To what is the limit set and by what?

Definition of terms. Most often it is a word which we define, and we define it by other words which attach a meaning to it. The result is a *term*, which comes from the Latin *terminus*, for it is the end of the line in which a meaning is stationed. A term has a particular meaning installed in it and it should be used in terms of that meaning, whereas a *word* may have many kinds of meanings. For example, we are at liberty to use the word "liberty" in many different ways, but Hobbes defines it as a term meaning the absence of external restraint (*Leviathan*, Pt. II, ch. 21). We should not read into Hobbes' term any other meaning associated with our uses of the word.

In definitions of terms there is a term defined (the *definiendum*) and the meaning assigned it (the *definiens*). By defining our terms we give sense to what we are talking about so that we can talk meaningfully about it. When I attended the University of Chicago its intellectual fighting cry was "Define your terms!"

Most definitions of terms in philosophy are accepted for the sake of discussion. What counts is where they lead us. The definition alone usually proves nothing. We may accept the definition of God as the all-knowing, eternal, omnipotent being, but that doesn't mean we are asserting that He or She exists. Such definitions are not conclusive. But a proof of God's existence will have to operate with some definition for God. Indeed, whenever we arrive at conclusions in philosophy we have relied on definitions along the way. Some definitions of terms are laid down in the course of the argument as distinctions instrumental to our advance. Thus, in proving that such a being as God does exist we may well have to define omnipotence, and much will probably hinge on the definition we have in mind for existence. Consider this rather brief proof: "I shall now prove God exists." "Good, go ahead." "I just did it." "I beg your pardon?" "Yes, God exists in my statement."

While a definition can be a neutral assignment of meaning to a term, bearing no surprises and raising no objections, a definition can also be a *commitment* to one meaning chosen from several possibilities. For instance, liberty may be defined following Plekhanov as "consciousness of necessity." [George Plekhanov, *The Role of the Individual in History* (New York: International Publishers, 1940), p. 16.] You may protest that he has taken liberties with the word and whatever conclusions he reaches in argument are tainted by such a partisan assignment of meaning. Yet you ought not to refuse to follow the rea-

soning because you do not accept its definitions. See what a Plekhanov or a Hobbes can do with his own definition. In philosophy
there is a liberty of defining things as may best conduct us to the
truth. An intellectual proverb has it: "There is no disputing definitions." Though this itself is open to dispute, we must concede the
philosophical right to assign meaning to *some* of our terms in order to
serve our insight or inquiry.

Conventional and invented terms. The freedom to define is not abso-
lute. There can be incorrect definitions. A unicorn, for instance, is
not a two-horned animal or a hornless animal but a one-horned animal. Yet, you protest, unicorns do not exist. That does not exempt
them from necessarily being one-horned. The explanation for this is
that unicorns are one-horned by definition (and by etymology). This
definition does not enter into the existential status of the subject, just
as defining God as omnipotent does not imply His or Her existence.
The definition of "unicorn" as one-horned is *conventional* and well established; that is, it is the generally agreed-upon sense of the word, as
attested by dictionaries. We must not abuse conventional meanings,
though we need not use them. Any change of definition from the ordinary must be made explicitly.

You can define a "zlerb" as a two-horned animal, or a particle of
matter, or a right of citizens, if you wish and if that helps your
argument. Since you will have been the only one to define a zlerb
there is no dispute. However, if what you are defining as a zlerb is already known by another name, such as rhinoceros or molecule or vot-
ing, then you may be misleading us or wasting your time. Sometimes
an argument can be kept clear of associations by asking the listener to
adopt a new technical term in place of an old controversial one. Thus,
"God," "liberty," and "happiness" may have so much emotion and
tradition packed into them as words that they are difficult for someone
untrained in philosophic reasoning to keep straight when defined as
terms. Fortunately, you are now training yourself to handle just such
difficulties.

Take care to distinguish between the use of a term and direct reference to the term itself. Liberty may have only two parts, while "liberty" has three syllables. When we mention a term rather than use it
we place it within quotation marks.

Some definitions of words, then, are correct by general usage and
are not usually disputed in philosophy. These are mostly names assigned to objects, real or imaginary, such as unicorns or tables and
chairs, or else they are the meanings of ordinary processes, such as

walking or growing. Then there are the stipulative or assumptive definitions whose correctness is open to dispute and which must be taken hypothetically. Most of the great issues in philosophy are of this kind: liberty, justice, beauty. In addition there are invented definitions which are uniquely assigned to unnamed things or processes. These are perforce indisputable but of rare occasion and limited utility. Try to do without introducing new terms if old ones can serve with suitable revision. But be wary of the accretions attached to older words which may mislead and cause needless dispute.

Though definitions of words are the simplest kind of definition and have been given the most attention in recent philosophic work in North America, it will not do to limit consideration of definition to words only, for the results may turn out more nominal than substantial. The story is told of Diogenes of Sinope that he responded to the definition current in Plato's Academy of man as "a featherless biped" by introducing a plucked chicken to the scholars. [Diogenes Laërtius, *Lives of Eminent Philosophers*, with trans. by R. D. Hicks (Cambridge, Mass.: Harvard University Press, "Loeb Classical Library," 1958), Vol. II, Bk. VI, 40, p. 43.]

Defining problems. Definition may be an identification by setting limits that mark off a field of inquiry. Definition can also be the narrowing into focus of a view; it may then be a plan for inquiry or an outline for procedure. Philosophers try to bring into sharp definition the thinking they engage in. Hence, definitions can not only get us going in philosophical reasoning and keep us going, but they can also be the *goal of our intellectual effort*. Definition may be the understanding of a subject or thing arrived at by a study of it. We are no longer dealing with the meaning of a word but with the meaning of some experience or thought, the meaning of a problem and its resolution. Thus, Plato's *Republic* written in ten "books" (i.e., chapters) may be conceived as a definition of justice, for that is the central concept inquired into and progressively clarified. The definition may not be located at any one point in the dialogue and formulated in a sentence. The definition as the delimiting of the problem and the narrowing down of its resolution takes place throughout the inquiry. Many of Plato's dialogues are studies in this kind of definition and you can learn from them how to pursue inquiry.

Philosophy can *arrive* at a definition in a chapter or an article. Many efforts on the great issues take this form. Thus, instead of starting with some definition of liberty, how would you go about *reaching* a reasonable or useful definition of it? To get somewhere you have to locate a context, analyze problems, pursue some distinctions, rely on other definitions, and advance an argument. Examine how Aristotle gathers the definition of tragedy in chapter 6 of the *Poetics* from his preceding analysis of the matter, history, and purpose of drama.

Responding to definition. When you encounter or advance a definition ask if it is an assumption, a conventional usage, a technical invention, a signpost, or a conclusion. By understanding its status you can appropriately use it, challenge it, accept it outright, take it hypothetically, or call for its verification.

Just as some students come to college with the notion that the answers to problems are to be found by looking them up in some book, so some beginners in philosophy turn to the dictionary to find out the truth about the issues discussed. But no problem of any substance in philosophy is resolved by looking it up in the dictionary (though Leibniz dreamt of a codified universal exact knowledge that could settle all philosophic disputes). The dictionary tells us how *words* are used. It will give conventional definitions and perhaps a selection of stipulated definitions. But that still leaves the burden of philosophy upon you to hypothetically follow out the stipulated ones, to stipulate others, and to arrive at definitions by inquiry. Despite its appearances, philosophy is not all words, words, words. Philosophy *is* a discursive art, often attired in weighty prose, but it aims to lay bare the truth, to broaden understanding, to resolve problems, to find meaning. Definitions that help in these endeavors belong in our philosophical work. Those that do not, though they mean well, are verbal exercises that mean little.

This entire discussion of definition is a partial definition which operates by analysis of purpose and by enumeration. The subject of definition is briefly studied in most introductory logic courses.

Principles. We have seen that definition may play the role of an initial commitment or a hypothetical claim in the argument that ensues. Every argument has a starting point, all reasoning has some foundation from which it proceeds. This beginning point is in the reasoning and need not be found at the outset of the discourse. It can be tucked away anywhere along the way and can even be tacit. The principal foundation of a line of reasoning or a theory we call a *principle* (see "principle" and "principal" in the Glossary, ch. 5). It may also go by the name of definition, assumption, hypothesis, premise, axiom, postulate, basic thesis, commitment, or foundation. There are different kinds of principles, and these names suggest different ways of conceiving of them.

In examining a philosophical argument, then, it is your duty to look for the principle. Ask: "What is the basic commitment here that is laid down so that the inquiry or the proof can proceed?" There is a stand taken—but on what grounds?—for a stand must have a footing somewhere. In this way you get to the *bottom of the argument*.

Methods.   If principles are the foundations of reasoning, definitions or distinctions its building tools, then *methods* are its construction. A method carries us forward. The word is from the Greek, meaning to go down a road. Definitions are boundary markers, principles are starting points, methods are routes of procedure, and conclusions are destinations. Those are the necessary components of a philosophic journey in any field. There is a variety of methods. In philosophy there is variety in everything that is important.

You must know *how you proceed* if you are to know where you stand and where you are going. The purpose of method is to get you somewhere. Methods do not stand still; you have no method unless you follow it. *Philosophic methods are not mechanical.* They require intellectual vigor in exploration, innovation, construction, and application. Though your method tells you what kind of step to take, you will have to spot the point at which to take that step.

Your responsibility as philosopher is to see to it that there is method to your reasoning. But that is not the whole duty. You are also responsible for recognizing the legitimate variety of methods available for treating problems. To dismiss the insights of Marx because he is a dialectician, or of William James because he examines problems in terms of performance and experience, is to close your mind to their contributions to philosophy, and thereby to close your mind to some of its own powers.

Method is known by other names, including procedure, approach, strategy, inquiry, and steps.

Forms of inference.   We have used "argument" to refer to the activity of philosophic demonstration or inquiry. A more general name for it is *reasoning*. In narrower terms argument may refer to any *form of inference* made within the course of the reasoning.

The study of the forms of *argument* and the standards to judge them is undertaken by logic. The possibilities of argument are enormous, for our mind is wonderfully resourceful in its powers of reasoning. Some of the scope and detail of those powers can best be appreciated by taking a course in logic or looking into a logic textbook. But even without such training or consultation you will have to develop some awareness of the logic of argument in your beginning philosophy course. (For discussion of logic as a branch of philosophy see ch. 2.)

You will have to detect the various kinds of argument as you go along. The instructor may have to draw these to your attention. You may have to draw them to his attention for analysis. The nature of argument is best perceived when one is in the midst of it rather than when one is abstractly instructed before reasoning commences in earnest. You will probably learn faster about the flowers and the weeds as you walk through the fields than by sitting in a room trying to master the entire botanical inventory. There, we have already had a form of argument in this paragraph. Did you grasp it? You may well have gotten the point of the piece of reasoning without recognizing what kind of reasoning it was. From now on you will abandon such habits of inattentiveness. You must not only get the point of the argument, you must also get the form, for the latter is what makes the former.

Analogy. The argument about flowers and weeds above is an *analogy*. An analogy asserts a *relationship* between two items which is *comparable* to the relationship evident between two better known items. The analogy claims that A is to B as C is to D. This may be expressed as a proportion or ratio in the form: $\frac{A}{B} : \frac{C}{D}$ in which $\frac{A}{B}$ and $\frac{C}{D}$ are called *analogues*. For an analogy to operate, one of its analogues must be acceptable without dispute; furthermore, the second analogue must have a relationship that is clearly comparable to the first. If these conditions are met, then a case has been made on behalf of the second analogue.

Put this argument in analogical form and fill in the missing step:

A watch is an ingenious article that operates regularly according to an intelligible pattern. It was, of course, designed to do so by the craftsman who contrived it with his intelligence and skill. The universe is far more marvelous in its operations but no less obedient to regular and intelligible law. Hence, . . .

Once you have figured out what this argument is, you may proceed to judge its soundness.

Analogical argument has notable features to its advantage and to its disadvantage. An analogy is not literal in its comparison; it is a similitude. Analogies take large comprehensive steps, as in the example above, where we move from a watch to the universe. Analogy is not deductive proof, but it may enlarge the understanding. It must be an easy argument to understand; otherwise it has lost its utility.

Argument by analogy is a favored technique of Socrates as he discusses the high notions of piety, justice, and virtue in terms of familiar activities. But one must have patience and willingness to see the connections. Callicles complains to Socrates in the *Gorgias* (491): "I swear you absolutely never stop talking about shoemakers and cleaners and cooks and doctors! As though our conversation were about them!" [Plato, *Gorgias*, trans. W. C. Helmbold (Indianapolis, Ind.: Bobbs-Merrill, "Library of Liberal Arts," 1952), p. 60.]

It has been said that every analogy, no matter how well it smooths the way to understanding, can be subjected to a counter-analogy or spoiled by a fly in the ointment. Thus, a watch stops completely before it is rewound but this we cannot say happens to the universe, so whatever is apparent about the watchmaker need not apply to the case of the universe. Since the two parts of the analogy, the watch and the universe, are only similar, one might always find that fly in the ointment which is their dissimilarity. And since there are endless kinds of similarity to be detected, we might well be able to construct an analogy for any case including the opposite to that which we had initially intended.

Induction. An analogy points to something similar in order to make a point by comparison. *Inductive argument* points to something observable in order to reach a general conclusion. It requires instances to give substance to its claims. But inductive claims are not mere descriptions of the few instances at hand; they are projections on the basis of what is at hand to cover other instances yet unknown. Induction is an important procedure in the observational sciences such as medicine and meteorology. In philosophy inductive argument is used to draw general consequences out of facts or experiences that individually are not in dispute.

For making inductive generalizations there are various criteria which are studied in logic and scientific methodology. Predictions made inductively cannot be certain; they are only probable. Induction, then, is an argument for the probability of generalizations holding for new instances. Induction too has its advantages and limitations. It relies on observables rather than on speculation, yet it can never reach all the pertinent observables and it may well miss those that would lead to different conclusions. That all swans are white was concluded on the basis of centuries of noting the color of individual swans. Then the black swan was discovered in Australia.

Where there are no observables or too few of them, induction will not tread. Probabilities may suffice for some matters, but philosophers are also given to a quest for certainty, which induction cannot satisfy.

Deduction. Deductive argument, by following certain formal rules, draws conclusions from claims already laid down. For the richness of forms that deduction may take, look into an introductory logic textbook, which usually gives the lion's share to deductive argument. We will mention some general features to look for in such argument.

Look for the conclusion in any line of argument. The conclusion is that which the reasoning is aiming at. Then look for the supporting claims from which the conclusion is drawn as consequence. Next identify the initial claims or premises that the intermediate steps are drawn from. Now by reversing the order of analysis you have the presentational form of deductive argument: premises, propositions (if any) based on the premises, conclusion based on all the foregoing. *Warning:* If you look first for the premises in a supposed piece of deduction you can be thrown off the track, for there may be extra premises present (red herrings) that do not contribute to the conclusion, or else the pertinent premises may be tacit and only discoverable by working back from the other explicit steps.

In any argument it is essential to keep clear what is being argued for (conclusion) and what the initial reasons (premises) are for that conclusion. If the premises are true and if the deduction is in the right form (valid), then the conclusion must be true. A deductive argument can only be valid or invalid, not true or false, while a conclusion can only be true or false, not valid or invalid. A conclusion may be validly arrived at if the argument is in the right form. *An argument will arrive at a true conclusion if it is in a valid form and employs true premises.* A valid argument, however, may lead to false conclusions. When?

Deduction is able to offer us a kind of certainty instead of probability. But where shall its true premises be found? From prior deductions—but then the same question is asked of them. From inductions—but these are only probably true. From intuitions—but these, it seems, cannot be argued for or against.

Intuition. We may define *intuition* as immediate knowledge given directly by the understanding without any intervening means such as premises, accumulated instances, or analogues. Intuition of a thing or fact does not require observation of it, as in induction, nor does intuition of a truth require formal reasoning, as in deduction, or comparison of relationship, as in analogy. There is no reasoning to intuition. No steps are taken to arrive at it or to justify it. Yet it has been claimed by philosophers, such as Aristotle, Descartes, and Bergson, that intuition reveals truth and is necessary to understanding. Other philosophers have tried not to rely on intuitions in their arguments because if one doesn't *have* the particular intuition discussed there seem to be no *steps* available for one to get it, nor may there be means for evaluating it.

Relationship of inference. A philosopher may spend much of his argument in a single form of inference. But one thinker is entitled to utilize all of them, for *the kinds of argument assist and complement one another.* It may be claimed that all induction rests on an intuition or is a deductive argument from the uniformity of nature, which allows one to connect instances and the unknown; that all deduction rests on intuition or induction for its premises, else it would have nothing to put its form upon; that analogies can be laid out convincingly to assist one to see similarities but cannot be taken for literal exactitude; and that intuitions give us literal exactitude but cannot be laid out as a form of reasoning. Whichever kinds or combinations of argument you encounter or use, be aware of their inherent shortcomings and recognize what resources are available in the other ways of arguing.

Ideas.   What about *ideas?* Ideas or concepts are most often the objects of philosophic thought. They constitute the intellectual awareness of something or they are mental constructs. But philosophy is not just a pack of ideas. It is the activity of thought. Ideas can result from such thinking or can play various roles within it. *Ideas alone do not constitute philosophy.* Characters on the stage and in literary works have lots of ideas, as do politicians and advertisers, but that does not make any of them philosophers. Ideas can be defined in order to make distinctions. An idea, such as matter or liberty, can be the heart of a principle. Arguments are often about ideas and they usually reach ideas as conclusions. A theory develops the full sense of an idea and usually relies on special ideas (theoretical concepts) for its functioning. A philosophy and a movement may turn on two or three important ideas.

How does one analyze and assess ideas or concepts, then, since they occur in varied contexts? *See the concept within its context,* and be aware of the context in which you reset the concept. "Context" is a concept worth your analysis and explanation. Part of the sense of the idea consists in what it is doing in the reasoning. Ignore the context and distort the sense; find the function and see the meaning. Ideas are alive only within thinking.

Your responsibility, then, for ideas is twofold: to understand what the idea does within the thinking in which it is presented and to understand what your thinking does to the idea. Get the idea? (For other ideas about ideas see the Glossary, ch. 5.)

Inquiry.   We discussed kinds of argument as presentations but they are also to be utilized as explorations. *Inquiry* proceeds not only by posing questions but by looking at instances, seeing where analogies might lead, following up the implications of premises, and probing subjects in the light of intuitions. Inquiry can begin with an idea and seek the ideas it is connected with, or inquiry can begin by seeking an appropriate idea for the commencement of reasoning in a particular area. What we have analyzed as methods are to be understood as methods of inquiry as well as methods of construction aimed at truth.

Socrates inquired into matters of human significance by questioning people who might know something of such matters. Plato constructed dialogues as inquiries into the identity of the true Ideas of things. Aristotle inquired into the causes or principles of things requiring different methods of study: nature, society, and art. Dewey studied inquiry as intellectual response to problems, thus making inquiry into inquiry. Kierkegaard turned inquiry onto faith, which resists formulation in any of the terms of inquiry.

Connection of problems.   If you have read some of the preceding chapters of this handbook you are already acquainted with the problem of problems in philosophy. Most of the book is devoted to getting you working on the problematic, for this is a beginning level of activity. Yet in your beginning course you may well have to move beyond treatment of particular problems. The problem with tackling problems one at a time is that by settling any one you may pose new difficulties for another. Though problems can be treated in isolation, they do not exist in isolation. You have to learn in philosophy that *problems are interconnected and the treatment of one has implications for the treatment of others.*

Theory.   The connected explanation and resolution of a set of problems in a field is a *theory.* Theories come in different sizes. The largest is that which covers an entire branch of philosophy. Thus, we may speak of Abelard's theory of logic, Hobbes' theory of politics, Hume's theory of knowledge. Such theories try to touch all the bases in the field. They are not theories of any one problem, though we may select for our study the treatment of any one problem by the theory. When you read a selection of this kind recognize that it is a part of a larger theoretical context. The way the problem at hand is treated may be due to the theory's treatment of related problems.

Book-length theories might not try to resolve all the problems in a field. It is enough of a contribution to get at the major difficulties, link them, overcome them, and point to the further application of the theory. Each theory takes certain problems to be predominant and makes others recede into secondary status. The central focus of one

theory is the marginal matter of another. Though theories are comprehensive, they are selective. Just as opposing treatments of a common
problem produce controversy, so whole theories may clash as alternative ways of treating an entire field. What should you look for, then,
in dealing with theories?

Determine the scope of the theory: What can it cover? The more a
theory can explain, the more powerful it is. Examine the theory's
choice of problems: What does it give importance to? What does it neglect? How does it identify the problem clusters? Ask on what
grounds and by what procedure the theory is constructed. What is the
argument for the theory? Where does it start, how does it advance,
where does it go? How well does the theory work when applied? Is it
flexible enough to handle problems not explicitly dealt with by its author? Is it "good in theory only but not in practice"? Kant wrote an
essay on this proverb, arguing that it cannot apply in philosophy. Is
the theory so complicated that it is too difficult to utilize? Simplicity
is often desirable in theories, though its significance has been over-
simplified. The criteria for theories can be conceived as: clarity, com-
pleteness, consistency, and applicability.

As you weigh theories against one another you will find that some
rate high in some respects but under other headings do not do as well
as others. Hence, it is your responsibility to revise theories where
revision is needed, patch and combine them, wrest the best from the
rest, or throw the whole bunch of them out and build a new one. Philosophy is often conceived as system-building, that is, as theory construction, rather than as problem-solving.

Don't hold back on thinking theoretically. Try to leap from the
particular problems studied to a whole field. A theory is a flight above
the field, which allows you to make sense of the terrain by seeing how
landmarks are related, where the obstacles are, and what the best
route is. As philosophers we want not only to crack problems as they
come upon us, but to be generally prepared with explanatory and ex-
ploratory apparatus. A triumphant settling of one issue might force a
disastrous outcome for another. A big problem in tackling any set of
problems is to determine the priority among issues and the locus of
value. Theories are sometimes invented as hypotheses before their
grounds are established or their consequences verified. They are "only
theories," but they might work. Often theories are offered and understood as sound alternatives for explaining or judging in a field though
not thereby the one correct way of doing so. A number of different
theories may each adequately treat the same subject.

Theories may be found in the smaller sizes as well, including the

theory of a few key problems in a field. One may even speak of someone's theory on a single important idea, as Leibniz's theory of mo-
nads, Locke's theory of majority rule, Abelard's theory of universals,
Buber's theory of I and Thou, but the full explanation of such ideas
would require the unfolding of a rather large theory. *Great ideas are really condensations of elaborate theories.* The idea is not defined in a sentence but explained in a volume.

A philosophy. You can identify the argument in a particular writing,
you can explore the theory of an author in some field, but what of the
connections between that author's work in one field and his work in
the other areas of philosophy? When we speak of a thinker's *philosophy*
we frequently mean his total set of contributions across the branches
of philosophy.

This is a concern for advanced courses in philosophy. Yet sometimes in a beginning course you will have the occasion to link up parts
of one philosopher's work. Thus, at different points in the term you
might read Plato on theory of knowledge, on justice, and on the arts.
You would assess each contribution in its place, but your duty is also
to bring these together as parts of one philosophy. In the case of
Plato, what we divide into separate branches is linked together by a
comprehensive view of the whole of knowledge and reality. We would
be unfair to Plato not to see his work on art, justice, and knowledge as
parts of this whole.

You may read Hume on knowing and Hume on morals. What is
the connection? Is the same method used? Are the same kinds of pre-
dicaments encountered? What about the difference between Aristotle's discussion of necessity in his *Physics* and his discussion of choice
in the *Nicomachean Ethics?* While you may have the chance to seek out
such connections, be on your guard, for some philosophers have no
integrated total philosophy operative in all branches. One of these
may tackle the different branches of philosophy as if he were a multitude of different philosophers. Such philosophers may even be incon-
sistent with themselves as they use methods or arrive at conclusions in
different branches. Locke and Russell have both been criticized for inconsistencies between their respective theories of knowledge and political writings. Sometimes a philosopher moves beyond his work in one
field to new work in another which makes the earlier contributions
outdated in his own eyes. Wittgenstein repudiated his early work
though it continues to be celebrated by Wittgensteinians. "Only connect!" as one of E. M. Forster's novels proclaims, but in your effort at
connecting be sure to spot the disconnections.

A movement.   In addition to identifying and dealing philosophically with one author's philosophy, it may be valuable to consider the *movement* or school (the *ism*) that he may belong to. The study of such movements is generally reserved for an advanced course, but you may be reading or discussing two or three thinkers who are British Empiricists, or Existentialists, or Pragmatists, or Logical Positivists, etc. Your duty is to consider the potentialities of a philosophy in relation to other philosophies. So you may have to deal with British Empiricism itself, in terms of what you see of it, rather than merely singly with Francis Bacon, Locke, Berkeley, Hume, or Russell. Again the caution is raised not to make links where there aren't any or where they would obscure the contributions of the individual thinkers. It is far too easy to apply the *ism* label (indeed, every philosopher can be accused of some *ism* or other) and thereby miss much of what is going on in the philosophy. One author's philosophical work can be enlarged by followers into an *ism* that may be active centuries after his death, e.g. Thomism (after Thomas Aquinas). I suppose there should be a special *ism* for philosophers who do not fit any *ism*. Marx is reputed to have said, "I'm no Marxist"; Freud claimed he was not a Freudian; the social thinker Robert Owen confessed he was not an Owenite. You take your chances when you seek the movement beyond the thinker, but then everything in philosophy has its risks.

Occasionally the instructor in a beginning course will refer to a particular thinker as a representative of an *ism*. You may encounter half a dozen or more *isms* this way. Don't fool yourself, or others, into thinking that you have indeed studied those movements. A sample does not make a movement. The instructor's purpose may be to sharpen the contrast between philosophies studied by assigning them striking names (an *ism* is impressive, isn't it?). Furthermore, by letting you know the label that is often tagged onto a certain kind of work in philosophy, the instructor or textbook writer gives you a tip on how to locate other philosophers who have done related work.

Shift in names.   In this chapter we have distinguished several levels of philosophic work, including definition, principle, method, argument, forms of inference, theory, a philosophy, and a movement. But these names are not to be taken as fixed and readily identifiable by all philosophy instructors or writers. They have been used here to mark certain *activities;* what counts is that you be able to recognize and conduct those activities. Be prepared to drop the labels and do the job. Don't quibble over words. When others speak of the argument, the method, or the philosophy, find out what they mean by these designations and see the value of what they are talking about.

As you practice these kinds of thinking you will find yourself more proficient at some than at others. You may be strong on working with method but weak in principles. You might have a keen eye for ideas yet not see an argument as a whole. Review of this chapter from time to time can help you find what you are missing so that you can put more work into it. Be reasonable in your expectations concerning reasoning, but understand that reasoning is perfectible only by reasoning.

Passages for study

1. *Socrates:* Don't let us be "misologues," hating argument as misanthropes hate men; the worst disease one can have is to hate arguments. [Plato, *Phaedo, Great Dialogues of Plato,* trans. W. H. D. Rouse (New York: New American Library, "Mentor Books," 1960), 89, p. 494.]

2. A definition is good when it is sagacious, and it is that when it so points the direction in which we can move expeditiously toward having an experience. [John Dewey, *Art as Experience* (New York: Capricorn, 1958), p. 216.]

3. The creed which accepts as the foundation of morals, Utility, or the Greatest Happiness Principle, holds that actions are right in proportion as they tend to promote happiness, wrong as they tend to produce the reverse of happiness. By happiness is intended pleasure, and the absence of pain; by unhappiness, pain, and the privation of pleasure. [John Stuart Mill, *Utilitarianism* (London: Parker, Son, and Bourn, 1863), ch. 2, pp. 9–10.]

4. And when I speak of the other division of the intelligible, you will understand me to speak of that other sort of knowledge which reason herself attains by the power of dialectic, using the hypotheses not as first principles, but only as hypotheses—that is to say, as steps and points of departure into a world which is above hypotheses, in order that she may soar beyond them to the first principle of the whole; and clinging to this and then to that which depends on this, by successive steps she descends again without the aid of any sensible object, from ideas, through ideas, and in ideas she ends. [Plato, *Republic,* trans. Benjamin Jowett (New York: Colonial Press, 1901), Bk. VI, 511, p. 207.]

5. Our discussion will be adequate if it has as much clearness as the subject-matter admits of, for precision is not to be sought for alike in all discussions, any more than in all the products of the crafts. . . . For it is the mark of an educated man to look for precision in each class of things just so far as the nature of the subject admits; it is

evidently equally foolish to accept probable reasoning from a mathematician and to demand from a rhetorician scientific proofs. [Aris-
totle, *Nicomachean Ethics*, trans. W. D. Ross, *The Oxford Translation of
Aristotle*, ed. W. D. Ross, Vol. IX (London: Oxford University Press,
1925), Bk. I, ch. 3, 1094^b.]

6. A reason is a *consideration which justifies:* to have a sufficient
reason for believing or for doing is to be justified in so deciding, and
to have no reason is to be unjustified and non-rational or irrational.
[Clarence Irving Lewis, *The Ground and Nature of the Right* (New York:
Columbia University Press, 1958), pp. 88–89.]

7. Our ideas reach no farther than our experience: We have no experience of divine attributes and operations: I need not conclude my
syllogism: You can draw the inference yourself. [David Hume, *Dialogues Concerning Natural Religion*, ed. Norman Kemp Smith (Indianapolis, Ind.: Bobbs-Merrill, "Library of Liberal Arts," 1947), Pt. II, pp.
142–143.]

8. Therefore, whatever is moved must be moved by another. If
that by which it is moved be itself moved, then this also must needs
be moved by another, and that by another again. But this cannot go
on to infinity, because then there would be no first mover, and, consequently, no other mover, seeing that subsequent movers move only
inasmuch as they are moved by the first mover; as the staff moves
only because it is moved by the hand. Therefore it is necessary to arrive at a first mover, moved by no other; and this everyone understands to be God. [Thomas Aquinas, *Summa Theologica, Introduction to
Saint Thomas Aquinas*, ed. Anton C. Pegis (New York: Modern Library, 1948), Pt. I, Q. 2, Art. 3, p. 25.]

Bibliography

1. Reasoning

Bacon, Roger. *Opus Majus*, trans. Robert Belle Burke, 2 vol. (Philadel-
    phia: University of Pennsylvania Press, 1928).
Comte, Auguste. *Introduction to Positive Philosophy*, trans. Frederick
    Ferré (Indianapolis, Ind: Bobbs-Merrill, "Library of Liberal Arts,"
    1970).
Descartes, René. *Rules for the Direction of the Mind*, trans. Laurence J.
    Lafleur (Indianapolis, Ind.: Bobbs-Merrill, "Library of Liberal
    Arts," 1961).
Hume, David. *Enquiries Concerning the Human Understanding and Con-
    cerning the Principles of Morals*, ed. L. A. Selby-Bigge (Oxford: The
    Clarendon Press, 2nd ed., 1951).
Kant, Immanuel. *Critique of Pure Reason*, trans. Norman Kemp Smith
    (New York: St. Martin's Press, 1965).

Peirce, Charles S. *Philosophical Writings,* ed. Justus Buchler (New York: Dover, 1955), especially "The Fixation of Belief" and "How to Make Our Ideas Clear."

Russell, Bertrand. *The Problems of Philosophy* (New York: Oxford University Press, "A Galaxy Book," 1959).

2. Movements

Ayer, A. J. *The Origins of Pragmatism* (San Francisco: Freeman, Cooper & Company, 1968).

The Empiricists: Locke, Berkeley, Hume (Garden City, N.Y.: Doubleday, "Anchor Books," 1974).

Kaufmann, Walter (ed.). *Existentialism from Dostoevsky to Sartre* (Cleveland: World Publishing, "Meridian Books," 1969).

Kockelmans, Joseph J. (ed.). *Phenomenology: The Philosophy of Edmund Husserl and Its Interpretation* (Garden City, N.Y.: Doubleday, "Anchor Books," 1967).

Mendel, Arthur P. (ed.). *Essential Works of Marxism* (New York: Bantam Books, "Bantam Matrix Editions," 1965).

The Rationalists: Descartes, Spinoza, Leibniz (Garden City, N.Y.: Doubleday, "Anchor Books," 1974).

5

Philosophical Language (with Glossary)

Living language. Philosophy does not require a special language. It is born in the living languages of the world and is borne by them. But as philosophy itself requires a refining of our thought, so it requires a special attentiveness in our use of language. Philosophy makes one self-conscious about words. Attend to what is being said if you want to know what is meant. Find out what is meant in order to know what is at stake. Philosophy looks for meaning in what we say, in the way things are said, and in what can be said. But let it not be said that philosophy is only words, for it is an art of speaking to problems by the use of reason.

Problems. Part of what constitutes a problem is the conception of it we set forth in words. *Most philosophic problems have a discursive dimension.* The phrasing of a question provides shape to an answer, and the stating of an answer not only responds to a question but gives leave for further questioning. So the philosopher thinks twice to determine what we are talking about, asking about, complaining about, or responding to. These are matters not of style but of sense.

In observing and probing of language the philosopher can find understanding, stimuli, and clues to the truth. We should bring these values to the fore in philosophic wording, making the most of the truth-enhancing features of normal language.

But the philosopher also observes in language a vast terrain of pitfalls: some disagreements are only quibbles over words; verbiage engenders pseudoproblems; questions can be improperly couched so as to defeat answering; answers may be high-sounding gobbledegook. A poorly stated position is poorly understood. Our thinking is oft betrayed by our tongue. There's many a slip 'twixt the mind and the lip. The philosopher's job is to eliminate deception, including self-deception, and to replace ambiguity with clarity. As philosopher, you should be cautiously aware of the truth-defeating features of language. You must strive for greater precision and more straightforwardness than you are accustomed to.

In his study of the idols or false notions that beset the understanding, Francis Bacon warns us:

> But the *Idols of the Market-place* are the most troublesome of all: idols which have crept into the understanding through the alliances of words and names. For men believe that their reason governs words; but it is also true that words react on the understanding; and this it is that has rendered philosophy and the sciences sophistical and inactive. [Francis Bacon, "The New Organon," *Works*, eds. James Spedding, Robert Leslie Ellis, and Douglas Denon Heath (New York: Hurd and Houghton), Vol. VIII (1869), Bk. I, No. lix, p. 86.]

Whereas heretofore you may have allowed words to "creep" into your understanding, now that you are philosophizing and are responsible for your understanding you must adopt critical standards for their admittance.

Etymology. A sign of the philosopher's sensitivity to the insights that are on the tip of our tongue is the abiding interest in etymology that extends from ancient times. Important words often have their roots embedded in profound meaning, such that the derivation of a word reveals the vitality of some theory. Etymology (what is the etymology of this word?) usually provides additional evidence or an elegant ornament to a proof in philosophy rather than a principal argument. But etymologies can be false or disputable, and misguided reasoning can twine itself around etymologies. Thus, when Freud claimed men as well as women suffer from hysteria, he was laughed at in medical circles because the Greek *hystera* means womb. [Sigmund Freud, *An Autobiographical Study*, trans. James Strachey (London: Hogarth Press, 1950), p. 25.]

Words and truth. How we say things is indicative of what things are to us. Words partake of the substance of human meaning, and in our words may be found our world. Meaning is suspended between word and world. Consider: Why is "being" a participle? What do you make of the fact that "virtue" comes from the Latin *vir* meaning "a man"? Why, instead of he or she, do we not call a person "it" as we do with other animals? Some philosophers, such as Heidegger, have sought the truth of being as revealed in language. The recent philosophic movement of ordinary language analysis re-examines the language of philosophic problems in the light of what is ordinarily meant by words. Other philosophers, such as Kierkegaard and Buber, explore the roots of the unspeakable as the grounds of truth; they have turned to words to suggest what cannot be said. "Upon that which we cannot speak, we should remain silent," says Wittgenstein as the mark of silence stamped on the last proposition of his *Tractatus* [Ludwig Wittgenstein, *Tractatus Logico-Philosophicus* (London: Routledge & Kegan Paul, 1961), prop. 7, p. 150.] But philosophers have frequently not honored this advice. They have sought to put into words what they have not been sure could be said. In the course of doing so they have said some things not previously understood. While philosophy aims for precision in the use of language, to be utterly precise, I fear, is to remain silent. In contradistinction to Wittgenstein we might say this is the rule of philosophy: *to attempt to tell the truth fully even though it be impossible for it to be told.*

Notice that a thorough consideration of the language of philosophy leads perforce to consideration of the philosophy of language. (See ch. 2 on areas of philosophy.)

Language and thinking.   Philosophy is a perpetual call for a more rigorous use of language, since ordinary usage falls short in constancy, sharpness, and disinterestedness. Because philosophy tries to clean up our thinking it obliges us to clean up our language. Language is present, of course, in our speaking and writing, as well as in our listening and reading. These are all forms of thinking, as we argue in the chapters of this handbook. But language is present in our thinking itself, for thinking is a form of language, or *language is the form of thought.* Thus, even when we think to ourselves, "language is essentially dialogue," to use the language of Ortega y Gasset. [José Ortega y Gasset, "Prólogo para franceses," *La rebelión de las masas* (Madrid: Revista de Occidente, 1962), pp. 5–6.]

Philosophical efforts.   Since ancient times philosophers have set into motion technical terms to accomplish things that ordinary words could not do, though many of these technical terms are former ordinary words that have been given a new and fixed sense. Philosophy has worked out an art or science of logic which teaches us not only proper reasoning but proper statement (the two appear to be inter-

dependent). "Logic" comes from the Greek *logos*, which variously means speech or reason. Perhaps as a consequence of logic's concern with the impurities of language, the greatest number of technical terms are found in this branch of philosophy. (See ch. 2 on logic as a branch.)

For centuries philosophy in the Western World had at its disposal a universal language of scholarship—Latin—which facilitated precise statement no matter what one's mother tongue. Philosophers still make use of the technical terms first laid down by the Greek philosophers in their struggle with words and of the Latin distinctions used in Roman, Scholastic, and early Modern times. Editions of Greek texts are today published with the notes and introductions in Latin, and the titles of Greek works are often cited in their Latin rendering (e.g., Aristotle, *De Anima*, "On the Soul").

The Romance languages, which are the offspring of Latin, merely modernized many of the philosophic distinctions of the parent tongue. English draws about half its vocabulary from Romance sources. Thus the very language in which we at present philosophize bespeaks a noble heritage which continues its life in our words. It seems our words spring from us, but it may also be said that we have our roots in words. In this century there has been a renewed call for a universal language of precise discourse, this time an artificial one tailor-made to the demands of rigor: symbolic logic. But to date symbolic logic has served more for the analysis of utterances than for their communication. (On "foreign" languages see ch. 3.)

Language and reasoning.   We are obliged, then, to make use of our language, profiting where we can from its insights but requiring it to serve us better than in its ordinary usage. Our first responsibility in using language philosophically is to stick to the philosophic: put aside the poetic, the dramatic, the lyrical, the emotive, the hortatory, the exclamatory, the imperative, the imperious, the defamatory, the inflammatory, the declamatory. What is left is philosophic discourse. So divested of the armory of linguistic powers it might seem destined to be dull. But it need not be, for philosophy speaks to the reason.

Language shall serve reasoning: that is the philosophic rule. Its values as entertainment, persuasion, or self-expression should not be allowed to interfere with this rule. In your speaking and writing, in your listening and reading, get to the reasoning. Reasoning takes substance in words, and you must therefore be attentive to the words. But do not think that the words before you are all there is to the reasoning. You must get through the words to the reasoning. Beginning students tend to stop at the surface of wording without examining the reasoning that informs the words. To put it in other words, you should think through what is involved and not just see, hear, and utter phrases. To detect what lies beneath the word you must attend to how the word is used. Words need not remain the same in their use but may enrich themselves with meaning as they move from context to context even within the same text. Plato especially illustrates this developing richness of meaning in his dialogues. See, for instance, the accretion of meaning to "virtue" in his *Meno*.

Practice. In the chapters on writing and examinations there are numerous hints on using language philosophically; here are some general practices for your work as philosopher. Don't waste words. They are precious. Our world is beset by a widespread pollution and waste of our intellectual resources, including language. Do your share to eliminate verbal garbage from your mind, your writing, and your speech. Conserve word power. Learning habits of economy in language will allow you to get more intellectual energy out of language as an instrument. That instrument serves you for the pursuit of truth. So that it may be worthy and fitting for such pursuit, your language should be cleansed of deception, hollowness, and nonsense. Break out from the shackles of popular phrases and accepted ways of saying things. Just as all your reasons come under critical scrutiny once you begin thinking philosophically, so all your phrases must be submitted to critical examination if you are to speak or write philosophically.

Here is the start of a verbal enema to bring forth what is not acceptable. "Let me say this": just say it. No one is holding you back except yourself. Similarly, "Let it be said that," "What I am saying is." There is no need to announce what you are doing when what you are doing is evident. Make sure that what you are doing is evident.

"In this argument I am not going to consider the following three points": don't dilate at length and in detail about what you are not going to do in your presentation; just go ahead and don't do it. It is assumed that you cannot deal with everything concerning the subject you are dealing with. What counts is what you do deal with.

"It goes without saying": a contradiction every time. "I shall be very brief and to the point": neither brief nor to the point.

Don't repeat; advance. Repeating a claim in different words does not make it true. In discussion there is precious little time to make any one point twice. In a term paper or exam there is no need to recall a previous claim to the reader, though this can be appropriate if you are writing a book. As I said before: repetition gets you nowhere.

Where something ordinary can be expressed in few words do so. Replace "He went on further to say" by "He continued"; "He then goes on to say" by "He says"; "I will try and explain" by "I will explain"; even better: drop the prefatory statement and explain. "Using this line of thought it can then be said": "Hence." "At this point I wish to object": "I object." "This would seem to indicate that": "This implies." "I adhere to the belief that": "I contend." "In the world we live in today": "In today's world" or just "Today." "With this in mind": but where else would it be if you have just called attention to it?

Be decisive. Take a stand. Pin down the issue. Settle the dispute. Don't be wishy-washy. Don't hedge, sidestep, backpedal, turn aside, or wiggle out of the problem. Banish such phrases as "I tend to agree." Your tendency is not enough to offer as philosophy; either you agree or you don't. Whichever it is, there are reasons to be offered for such a stance and usually objections to be raised. Give your reasons and answer the objections. Be specific as to what in a position rational people ought to agree with (for this is what you often mean by saying, "I agree with it"). Don't be sweeping and vague as in this closing line of a student paper: "I am for the most part in accord with the philosophy but perhaps not too [*sic*] such a great degree."

The following statements are inadmissible as judgments in philosophy:

I pretty much feel Nietzsche is right.
The objection to materialism seems sound.
The causality proof of God sounds valid to me.
In my opinion, determinism rules out any freedom of the will.
Personally, I believe happiness is doing good to others.

These are not genuine commitments concerning the reasons for things. They are observations on how things appear (appearances are deceiving) or else they are expressions of your attitudes (attitudes may be wrong). A certain modesty and hesitation to be forthright may lead you to garb your ideas in these cloaking phrases. Cast them off: bare your thoughts. Be true to thine own mind.

See what happens when you state your judgments straightforwardly:

Nietzsche is right.
The objection to materialism is sound.
The causality proof of God is valid.
Determinism rules out any freedom of will.
Happiness is doing good to others.

They gain in force and clarity as they are simplified and made direct. They arrest the intellect instead of letting its attention float off. Notice that such decisive statements not only get your point across but they call for reinforcement. By hitting the point you place yourself on the spot. Mere assertion without supportive reasons is dogmatism. Philosophy begins when you commence reasoning for the claims you make. Thus, your responsibility in making the above claims is to:

explain how Nietzsche is right,
show why the objection to materialism is sound,
demonstrate the validity of the causality argument,
prove that determinism is incompatible with freedom,
and give the reasons for doing good to others as constituting
    happiness.

Those are big tasks. But they are the very kinds of tasks that philosophizing involves. As you make bold claims and begin to back them up you will be aware that such claims are debatable. That is why you have to back them up. That they are debatable makes them worth debating. Don't shy away from argument; it is the lifeblood of philosophy. Be willing to take a chance on arguing for your ideas. Judgments in philosophy need supporting, not mere reporting.

Quotation.   A quotation is a passage that is quoted. In making a quotation you quote. A quotation is visually signaled by quotation marks: " ". In speech you can indicate when you are quoting by a pause and change of intonation, or else by saying at the beginning "quote" or "open quotes" and at the conclusion "end of quotation" or "close quotes." Do not make signals in the air with your fingers, for that is distracting. You are responsible for making perfectly clear when you are quoting anything and when you cease to quote it. Note: the term "a quotation" is popularly being replaced by "a quote."

Quotation marks are to be used when referring to words as distinct from what the words refer to. For example, "Philadelphia" is larger than "Tokyo," although Tokyo is larger than Philadelphia. Quotation marks are also used to emphasize the special or suspect meaning of terms (in speaking, use special intonation), e.g. Plekhanov's theory of "freedom" as necessity, Tillich's analysis of "ultimate concern." When something is eliminated from a quotation (an ellipsis) it is signaled by a series of dots, generally three: . . . (for more on quotation in writing see ch. 6).

Technical terms.   There are technical terms in the language of every discipline. These special words place emphasis on things important to that discipline which are not adequately expressed in ordinary words. Technical expressions can condense a useful line of thought or even a theory into a term that serves as a shortcut. Technical terms can be invented in pairs or groups to enforce contrasts or make relationships clear. Technical terms, then, are intended to be conveniences for speaking within a field. Yet they often prove inconvenient due to abuse or failure to master them. Technical terms are abused when used to obscure. In my earlier days as a lecturer, a professor advised me: "When you have nothing to say put it in technical terms."

Don't use special terms to make things more difficult; they are intended to make things easier. To escape from under the stifling weight of established technical terms philosophers often propose new technical terms.

Another abuse consists in merely parading the fancy words without putting them to use. That you have stated a problem in technical language does not mean that you have dealt with it. If you can say something just as well in ordinary words do so. The less technical your philosophic language the wider the range of people who can discuss the problems with you.

But be prepared to recognize the meaning of special philosophic terms when they occur, for most philosophers will not stop to explain all the terms of their trade. They will assume you understand the philosophic vocabulary. This means that you have to look things up. Most of these words, due to the interesting history of Western philosophy, are of Greek and Latin origin. They may look strange, sound difficult, and be multisyllabic. All the better, since this makes them stick out like a sore thumb. When you see one of these, like "epiphenomenalism," you *know* that you don't know what it means. Hence, you consult a reference work. It is a good idea to examine the etymology of big philosophic words, for the roots will give sense to the strange word and will help in explaining other words.

Every philosopher has the privilege of offering a technical term for his own theories. Certain terms are recognized as the special coinage of a particular thinker and you would have to see how that thinker gives them meaning. Among the famous ones: Bergson's *élan vital*, Kant's synthetic *a priori*, Leibniz's monad, Husserl's *epoché*, Occam's razor, Pascal's wager, Nietzsche's will to power, Rousseau's general will, James' will to believe.

Some technical expressions in philosophy are words from other languages for which there are no English equivalents but which have even become English words. These you can locate in an English dictionary or a philosophical reference work. A few of the notable ones: from German, *Angst*, a dread without specific object; from Greek, *hubris,* an excess of pride; from Sanskrit, *Nirvana,* culminating enlightenment and peace; from Chinese, *Tao,* the path of moral or cosmic law.

The Glossary includes three kinds of entries. (1) There is a listing of a dozen or so foreign *phrases* that you might not find in a general dictionary but are likely to encounter in philosophic discussion and reading. An example is the doctrine *esse est percipi.* These items are simply translated and given an authorial identification where appropriate.

(2) There are a dozen or so listings of terms special to philosophy, those technical terms, like "tautology," that you have probably not encountered before but which are in everyday use in philosophy. You should become aware of these sooner or later. They are tricky and can mislead you unless you fix their sense clearly in your mind. The selection here is limited to terms so widespread in philosophy that your instructor and your textbook author might not even think them special and hence not stop to explain them.

(3) But the greatest number of entries in the Glossary consists of words that *ordinarily* have other connotations than their peculiar philosophic usage. These words you might not even notice as being technical, and hence you might not think it appropriate to look them up. As a result you might miss the philosophic point. Thus, you know what the ordinary word "immediate" means; indeed, doesn't its mention immediately bring to mind its sense? But in philosophic usage there is a much sharper sense assigned the term which contrasts it with the mediate. Be prepared to find in philosophy that love need not be an emotion but can be a spiritual or intellectual commitment; that feeling need not be an emotion but can be a mode of apprehending; that passion is suffering or being acted upon as opposed to action; and that "some" in logic may mean as few as one and as many as all.

You will have to be alert to detect the special usage of ordinary words. You will have to be willing to ask about or look up a word that you seem to know. The Glossary is designed not only to be consulted when you have such a word in mind but to be read through or glanced at when you have the time so that you can become familiar with the troublesome words in advance.

Wherever possible in the entries for the special terms and the technical use of ordinary terms, related terms have been discussed together. In this way you may discover *a set of distinctions* and recognize where opposites are drawn. Words that look or sound alike and are easily confounded are distinguished here. The Glossary, then, is designed to help your overall understanding of philosophic language as well as your grasp of specific philosophic problems. For specific uses by specific authors you will have to consult those authors or full-length reference books.

I hope philosophy has many a good word for you!

Passages for study

1. The big problem with philosophers and their writings is that on the whole they use fancy words, long sentences, with lots of foreign words, e.g. German, lots of commas, semi-colons, etc. which looks impressive and formidable. When you read it and it doesn't make any sense you think how profound these men must be to be able to write such "truths." Their lack of ability to write in a clear meaningful manner sometimes leads me to believe that they are nothing but [expletive deleted] *par excellence*. Philosophy may have something to contribute to the development and education of the student, but all of this is lost if it cannot *communicate* these ideas. [Student comment.]

2. Philosophical discourse is the common conversation of mankind raised to the highest degree of elegance and precision. [Mortimer J. Adler, "The Philosopher" in *The Works of the Mind*, ed. Robert B. Heywood (Chicago: University of Chicago Press, 1947), p. 230.]

3. To this inquiry the foregoing discussion respecting the meaning of terms, was an indispensable introduction. Language is as it were the atmosphere of philosophical investigation, which must be made transparent before anything can be seen through it in the true figure and position. [John Stuart Mill, "Nature," *Three Essays on Religion* (New York: AMS Press, 1970), p. 13.]

4. Philosophy lives in words, but truth and fact well up into our lives in ways that exceed verbal formulation. [William James, *The Varieties of Religious Experience* (New York: Modern Library, 1902), p. 446.]

5. All philosophy is, therefore, at bottom philology. [Miguel de Unamuno, *Tragic Sense of Life*, trans. J. E. Crawford Flitch (New York: Dover, 1954), p. 311.]

Bibliography

Austin, J. L. *How to Do Things with Words* (Cambridge, Mass.: Harvard University Press, 1962).

Ayer, Alfred Jules, *Language, Truth and Logic* (New York: Dover, no date).

Belaval, Yvon. *Philosophers and Their Language*, trans. Norbert Guterman (Athens, Ohio: Ohio University Press, 1966).

Blanshard, Brand. *On Philosophical Style* (Bloomington, Ind.: Indiana University Press, "A Midland Book," 1967).

Ogden, C. K., and Richards, I. A. *The Meaning of Meaning: A Study of the Influence of Language upon Thought and of the Science of Symbolism* (New York: Harcourt, Brace & World, "A Harvest Book," no date).

Plato. *Cratylus*.

Note: For philosophical dictionaries consult the reference works listed in ch. 8. Other aids to language are listed in ch. 6 on writing. On the philosophy of language see "Other Branches," listed in ch. 2.

Glossary

abstract, see "intangible"

absurdity, *reductio ad absurdum*

"Absurdity" generally refers to something lacking in meaning, self-contradictory, or else impossible. Hence, absurdities are usually to be avoided in philosophy, which seeks the meaningful, the true, and the real. Some philosophers, notably Existentialists, assert that there may be no meaning and that man's reality is fundamentally absurd. Lat.: *ab* + *surdus*, "from the surd," that which is not rationally analyzable. What, then, is a mathematical surd?

A *reductio ad absurdum* is a refutation of an argument that "reduces it to absurdity" by showing that it would lead to fantastic conclusions.

accept, except

These words are sometimes carelessly exchanged in writing. To accept an idea is to concur in it. To raise exceptions is to make a special case for something or to make objections against it. Accept your responsibility for clarity and take exceptional care with such tricky words.

accidental, see "essential"

action, see "passion"

actual, potential

"Actual" ordinarily means what is true or factual. In philosophy the actual may be thought of as the realization (see "realize") of the potential, which itself may be true in some sense. Thus, there is someone actually riding a bicycle across the campus, though before he started he was only potentially a rider of the bike. Yet because he was potentially a bike-rider, he was able to actualize the bike-riding.

affect, effect

These words are frequently mixed up in ordinary writing. It is time for you to keep them straight. An effect is the result of a cause; an affect is a feeling. To effect is to bring about or cause; to affect is to influence or to feign. Something affective is emotive (see "passion," "feeling"); something effective works well. The antonym of "effect" is "cause." So that your verbal discrimination will be effective don't let yourself be adversely affected by the con-

87

fusion of terms. Figure this one out: "Every Cause has an affect, but every cause has an effect."

ambiguity, ambivalence, equivocation

Where two or more different senses are contained in a phrase or argument there is an ambiguity (Lat.: *ambi*, "both"). An ambiguity is a confounded meaning (confound it!). Philosophy, unlike poetry, finds ambiguities undesirable; it is the philosopher's mission to resolve ambiguities wherever he finds them in reasoning.

An ambivalence in a person or a passage is an indecisiveness that sways one way and the other on a particular point, e. g. if you have a love/hate attitude toward college you are ambivalent. Ambivalent arguments are not tolerated by logic. Do you see why?

Ambiguities are unintentional as may be ambivalences, but equivocations are generally deliberate. The equivocation gives "equal voice" in one expression to two opposed positions. This is not playing fair philosophically.

ambivalence, see "ambiguity"

amor intellectualis Dei

Lat.: "intellectual love of God." (Spinoza)

analytic proposition, see "proposition"

anomaly, antinomy

Anomaly (Gr.: *an*, "against," + *nomos*, "law") is something that goes against a law or set of rules. It sticks out like a sore thumb amidst explanatory theory and invites further exploration. That upland geese have webbed feet is an anomaly that Darwin holds against the theory of an independent creation of each species.

A related word, with the same Greek roots, is "antinomy," which refers to some rule or claim that goes against the grain of another rule or law. It is a contradiction of principles. One of the greatest of antinomies is: "All events in nature are causally determined," "Man is free."

antinomy, see "anomaly"

antithesis, see "thesis"

a posteriori, see *a priori*

a priori, *a posteriori*, empirical, Empiricism

A priori is a Latin expression, generally italicized, which has become part of the English language and is of frequent use in philosophy. It means that which is known independently of experience. Kant argues that the principles of morality are known *a priori*.

The antonym is *a posteriori*, meaning knowledge that follows from or is dependent upon experience. Another antonym is "empirical" (Gr.: *empeiria*, "experience"). Locke, a proponent of Empiricism, claims that all our knowledge is empirical. Empiricism is opposed to Rationalism in its mode of pursuing truth.

becoming, see "being"

being, becoming, nothing, null set

Ordinarily, "a being" refers to an existent thing, such as a table, an animal, or a human. Together, these things are an accumulation of beings, but philosophy may ask, "What is being itself that entities partake of or exemplify?" This problem of being, existence, or reality is studied by the branch of metaphysics called ontology (Gr.: *onta*, "being") (see ch. 2).

While being may be contrasted with beings, it may also be contrasted with becoming. "Becoming" may refer to the real as process rather than as substance or entity. Process philosophers, such as Whitehead, direct our attention to emergence or the immanent, rather than to fixed form or substance. For Plato the realm of being, of Forms or Ideas, is the "really real," while the realm of becoming, which is the world of matter and change, is delusory.

Another philosophic contrast to being is found by thinkers in nothing or nothingness. Nothing can be not simply the absence of being but the silent partner which allows being to be. Thus, if one is to properly understand being, in some sense one must have nothing in mind, claim Lao Tzu and Heidegger. In logic nothing is expressed as the null set, that is, a set which has no members.

being philosophical, see "philosophizing"

being rational, see "rationalize"

binary relation, see "dualism"

categorical, see "category"

category, categorical

In ordinary usage a "category" is a heading under which things can be listed. Philosophy takes categories quite seriously, seeking the fundamental ways in which everything is identifiable and groupable. Philosophic categories are ultimate classifications.

The categorical is the unconditional. It is opposed to the contingent and the hypothetical (see "hypothesis"). Kant's categorical imperative is a command that brooks no ifs, ands, or buts.

cause, efficient cause, final cause, proximate cause, first cause, chain of causality

"Cause" ordinarily means that which brings about an effect due to its action, as a frisbee's flight is caused by your throwing it. The ordinary sense, as just described, is known in philosophy as the "efficient cause." Other causes of the event, as analyzed by Aristotle (*Metaphysics*, Bk. V, ch. 2, 1013ª-1014ª), include the formal, material, and final cause.

The "final cause" does not mean the last cause mechanically operative immediately before the event (that would be the proximate cause), but the purpose or end that gives guidance to the process. Thus, the final cause of the frisbee's flight may be a desire to entertain yourself in the company of your friends.

The first cause is that cause which is not an effect of any other cause but which is required for there to have been any effect. Problem: What, then, accounts for the first cause?

The "chain of causality" refers to each effect having a cause which in turn requires a cause. In other words, events are strictly determined and do not occur spontaneously. Problem: Does the chain of causality require that there be a first cause? If so, isn't that first cause outside the chain and an anomaly?

Some causes do not merely bring events about but sustain things in their existence. (See "determinism," *ex nihilo nihil fit*, "ultimate" and related terms.)

chain of causality, see "cause"

cogito ergo sum

Lat.: "I think, therefore I am" (Descartes). This argument is frequently referred to in philosophy as "the *Cogito.*"

concept, see "idea"

conditional proposition, see "imply"

conscience, see "conscious"

conscious, conscience, unconscious, subconscious

"Conscious" and "conscience" derive from the same Latin verb, *scire*, "to know." They are occasionally interchanged in ordinary speech, and ambiguities are generated when the second syllable is slurred. To be conscious of something is to be aware of it, to be awake to it. Consciousness is the state or process of the subject's awareness. You may be conscious not only of objects but of subjective conditions such as pleasure, desire, will. It is often argued in philosophy that consciousness is a precondition for knowledge.

The "conscience" refers to scruples felt by the subject. These are generally moral limits that an inner voice dictates to the person. It may be argued that conscience is a kind of knowledge of the highest principles of conduct; it may also be argued that conscience is but the stern echo of the values of those who saw to one's upbringing. We have the opportunity to make ourselves conscious of our conscience, and conscience may make us conscious of our duty. In any event, a conscientious philosopher keeps these distinctions clear in his consciousness.

There is unconscious knowledge, according to Freud—that is, a knowing or believing that our conscious mind is ordinarily unaware of. The term "subconscious," which Freud objected to but which is widespread, may refer to the unconscious or else to what lies just below the surface of awareness. The exploration and expansion of consciousness have been the task of several important methods, including Psychoanalysis, Phenomenology, and Yoga.

contingent condition, see "necessary and sufficient condition"

contradiction, see "dilemma"

contradictory, see "dilemma"

contrary, see "dilemma"

deduction, see "induction"

de gustibus non disputandum est

Lat.: "There is no disputing matters of taste." Proverb often cited—and disputed—in aesthetics.

determinism, predetermination, fatalism

Determinism is the theory that for every natural effect there is a regular cause. Spontaneous uncaused events or randomness are ruled out. A determinist holds to the law or chain of causality. A predeterminist goes further than that, asserting that events have been planned in advance to occur through the chain of causality. "Predetermination" or "predestination" are terms used for this foreordainment, generally attributed to God as the all-knowing first cause. A fatalist believes there is no sense in trying to change the course of events since they must necessarily take place in accordance with a scheme beyond our control. Roughly speaking, determinism refers to causal mechanism, predetermination involves purposeful foreknowledge (see "teleology"), and fatalism refers to the problem of action. (See "cause" and related terms, "indeterminism" and related terms.)

deus ex machina

To pull a rabbit out of a hat. In argument it means to hit upon some almost magical device to get one out of a difficulty. The Latin phrase refers to the theatrical device of having a god pop out of the scenery.

dialectic, Dialectical Materialism

The words "dialectic," "dialectics," and "dialectical" in their original and largest sense refer to the art of philosophic discussion. Hence, every philosopher ought to be skilled in dialectic. Dialectic is a branch of the Scholastic *trivium* or liberal arts. "Dialectic" may also mean working from opinions in philosophic exploration rather than strict demonstration. There is a yet more specialized sense in which "dialectic" refers to a certain kind of process in discourse or in history, the Hegelian dialectic or the Marxist Dialectical Materialism, which arrives at the synthesis of antithetical positions (see "thesis").

Dialectical Materialism, see "dialectic"

dichotomy, see "dualism"

dilemma, paradox, contradiction, contradictory, contrary, self-contradiction

A dilemma is a special kind of quandary: it is a trap in which either of the two seeming ways out is unsatisfactory. One is caught "between the horns" of a dilemma (Gr.: *di +lemma*, "two legs or branches") and there is no straightforward solution. You're damned if you do and damned if you don't.

A paradox is a puzzle of a proposition which appears to deny itself, as "This statement is not true." A paradox defies determination as true or false; rather, it begs to be straightened out in a new formulation. Paradoxes often stimulate thought to explore fundamental problems with refreshed curiosity, as has been the case with the paradoxes of Zeno.

A contradiction is a denial of a proposition such that the proposition and its contradiction cannot both be true or both false. In other words, claims that are contradictory are opposed such that if one is true the other is false. For example, if "it is not raining" is true, then its contradictory, "it is raining," is false.

In logic we distinguish other kinds of opposition between claims, including contraries. Two claims are contrary if they both cannot be true although they both might be false. Thus, "all dogs are pets" is the contrary (not the contradictory) of "no dogs are pets." Both claims deny one another, but both are false.

A contradiction can be tucked into the very claim one propounds. If sufficiently puzzling this is a paradox and is to be resolved, if simply erroneous it is a self-contradiction and is inadmissible. We also speak of a "contradiction in terms" when we violate the very sense of the words we are using, as in "a married bachelor."

ding-an-sich
Ger.: "The thing in itself," as distinct from the representation of the thing in our consciousness, the real thing rather than the apparent object or phenomenon. Kant underscored the subject's predicament in learning of the thing in itself. (See "noumenal," "transcendental.")

doing philosophy, see "philosophizing"

dualism, dichotomy, binary relation, dyadic relation, monism
What is dual, binary, or dyadic is twofold. In philosophy "dualism" generally refers to the metaphysical position that being is composed of two substances—say, matter and mind. It is distinguished from monism, which holds to a single substance. Berkeley is a monist (mind), Democritus is also a monist (matter), but Descartes is a dualist (mind and matter). Other dualisms are spoken of in ethics (good and evil) and theory of knowledge (subject and object).

"Dichotomy" is a fancy word for a division of something into two parts. In metaphysics there is a dichotomy of Materialism and Idealism.

In logic a binary relation is one that applies to two parties, e.g. "The sun is larger than the earth." This is also called a "dyadic relation." Relations connecting three parties are triadic.

dyadic relation, see "dualism"

effect, see "affect"

efficient cause, see "cause"

eminent, see "immanent"

empirical, see *a priori*

Empiricism, see *a priori*

end, teleology

   In addition to meaning the stopping or termination of something, "end" may mean its culmination, fulfillment, goal, or perfection. Hence, a discussion of the end of life is likely to be about happiness rather than death. The Greek term is *telos*, from which we get "teleology," the study of purpose in the universe. The teleological is the purposive. (See "final cause," "predetermination," "will.") Much work in philosophy consists of distinguishing ends from means and conceiving appropriate means for given ends.

ends-means continuum, see "mean"

entailment, see "imply"

epiphenomenalism, see "phenomenon"

equivocation, see "ambiguity"

esse est percipi

   Lat.: "To be is to be perceived," that is, something takes its existence in its being perceived (Berkeley).

essential, accidental, existential, Existentialism

   In ordinary speech something "essential" is quite important, and something "accidental" is a chance occurrence that may be harmful. Philosophy gives a more rigorous sense to these terms that turns them into useful opposites. Thus, the "essential" refers to the essence of something, that is, what necessarily is intrinsic to it. The essence is what something is. The "accidental" refers to the qualities that adhere to but are not necessary to the thing discussed. For example, the engine is essential to my automobile but the car's color is only accidental. Philosophy and science aim to know the essence as distinguishable from the accidents.

   In another sense, the essence of something is its definition or the concept of it, and this may be contrasted with its substance or existence. The existential is substantial, while the essential is conceptual. Sartre claims as a principle of Existentialism that for man existence precedes essence: explain his point.

eternal, see "infinite"

except, see "accept"

existential, see "essential"

Existentialism, see "essential"

ex nihilo nihil fit

   Lat.: "Nothing comes from nothing." The point is that what *does* exist has followed from some cause. The proverbial claim is important to proofs of God's existence by urging the necessity of a first cause. Also: *nihil ex nihilo*.

experimentum crucis

   Lat.: "The decisive experiment," an experiment so devised as to shatter a theory or conclusively verify it (Francis Bacon).

extension, see "intention"

fatalism, see "determinism"

feeling
   "Feeling" is a rather rich word in life and philosophy. It may be an emotion or passion: "I feel sad"; a report of a subjective (see "subject") state: "I feel well"; a tactile sense of what is tangible (see "intangible"): "I feel the chair." Feeling or sentiment may also be an affective (see "affect") way of knowing, that is, a sensing in subjective terms of an objective (see "object") state of affairs. This latter sense is especially important in aesthetics.

final cause, see "cause"
first cause, see "cause"
free will, see "will"
golden mean, see "mean"
hypothesis, see "thesis"
hypothetical proposition, see "imply"
idea, ideal, Idealism, concept
   You already have some idea of what the word "idea" means, and you will surely be encountering many a strange idea in philosophy. Philosophy gives us ideas. There are some special senses to be noted. "Idea" is a Greek word which means "form." An idea of something is a form, not necessarily its shape, but the structure of its identity, whether that something is a table or justice. Plato's theory of Ideas or Forms (generally capitalized) attributes the greatest reality to certain pure ideas which things around us merely participate in or else are the images of. In Hegel's theory of history Ideas realize themselves in Nature. For Kant and other philosophers an Idea is a regulative principle or criterion.
   "Idealism" (note the *l*) as a philosophical movement concerns itself with such theories of ideas as realities or standards. Note that "ideal" can serve as the adjective to "idea," though "mental" is more commonly used. Idealism in philosophy is not necessarily the praise of noble values but the theory of mental substance. It is opposed to Materialism.
   "Idea" and "concept" are ordinarily interchangeable, but sometimes they are distinguished (as by Hegel) in that the concept is created by the thinker (conceptualized), whereas the idea may have an existence in reality (ideational).

ideal, see "idea"
Idealism, see "idea"
immanent, imminent, eminent, transcendental
   Someone eminent is outstanding, something imminent is on the verge of happening, something immanent is inherent within a process or entity and will emerge from it. Imminency refers to temporality, but immanency refers to internality. An eminent thinker warned: the immanent need not be imminent.
   The antonym of "immanence" is "transcendence." "Transcendental" is a very big word for that which goes beyond. A transcen-

dental God would be one outside our experience or world. Transcendental knowledge would go beyond our ordinary, say empirical, sources of knowing. Transcendental does not imply nonexistent. Warning: in Kant there is a difference between the transcendental, which is *a priori*, and the transcendent, which is unknowable, such as the *ding-an-sich*.

immediate, mediate, intermediate

In ordinary speech to do something immediately is to get it done pretty damn quick. Yet some seconds do elapse before we actually attend to most "immediacies." In philosophy we use the word with literal exactitude. The immediate experience has no mediation, no middleman, so to speak, between your awareness as subject and the object of the experience. Immediate knowing is direct knowledge unassisted by reasoning (see "intuition," "mystical"). Whether there is any immediate experience and whether there is any immediate knowledge are questions probed by philosophers. Most knowledge is mediate, that is, arrived at by means of intermediate stages.

imminent, see "immanent"

implication, see "imply"

imply, infer, implication, inference, entailment, hypothetical proposition, conditional proposition

"Imply" and "infer" are sometimes mixed up in ordinary discourse. To imply is to put forward a suggestion or conclusion which may be incompletely stated, while to infer is to draw forth a conclusion from statements or evidence. Thus, by this entry I am implying that it is worth your while to grasp this distinction, and you may infer from its presence that you will profit from it. In addition to these common senses, philosophy may place more rigorous standards for usage of the terms, insisting that inference and implication be logical steps and not just suggestions or surmises. Logic itself is the art of inference. Please explain what this implies.

An implication in symbolic logic is a proposition of a certain form—"if p then q," "p implies q," or "$p \supset q$"—also known as a conditional or hypothetical proposition or entailment.

indeterminism, principle of indeterminancy, uncertainty principle, randomness

Indeterminism is the belief that not all events involving persons are strictly determined by the chain of causality operative in the natural world. Thus, it is opposed to determinism and opens the door to free will. Indeterminism recognizes the freedom of the will as a cause in the world, while determinism usually sees the activities of the will as effects of the world.

The principle of indeterminancy (also known as the "uncertainty principle"), propounded by Heisenberg, refers to the predicament of being unable to measure some features of a phenomenon without interfering with other measurable features of it. It is *we* who cannot, in principle, determine the parameters of the phenomenon. Indeterminism is not a blanket denial of causality, and indeterminancy is not an assertion of undetermined events.

The lack of causal chains is randomness. Randomness in ethics and teleology is lack of purpose. In mathematics randomness is a process of selection .bound by no special probabilities. Be determined to keep these nuances clear and not let your understanding rest on uncertainty and chance.

induction, deduction

Induction is the reasoning that proceeds from particulars to general claims. Inductive logic is empirical. Deduction is the reasoning that proceeds from general propositions to other propositions either general or more particular. Deductive logic is not empirical but formal—that is, the form and not the content of its propositions lead to inferences. Problem: Is the distinction between induction and deduction an inductive or deductive one? (For further discussion of induction and deduction see ch. 4 on philosophic reasoning, and the discussion of logic in ch. 2.)

infer, see "imply"

inference, see "imply"

infinite, eternal

In ordinary speech "infinite" can refer to something astonishing and beyond comprehension. Literally, the infinite (Lat.: *in*, "without," +*finitus*, "boundary") has no limit; it is boundless. That does not mean it is undefinable or unreal. Indeed, it has just been defined. Infinity may have a mathematical sense or a physical sense. There is a world of difference between a number that is infinite and a universe that is infinite.

The eternal is the infinite in time, that is, time without end. (See *sub specie æternitatas*.)

initial, see "ultimate"

intangible, abstract

The word "intangible" frequently is applied in a pejorative sense in ordinary speech to what is vague, nonexistent, or imaginary. Literally, the intangible is that which cannot be touched. Often in philosophy you will deal with such intangibles, which may be clear and real, such as ideas.

"Abstract" is sometimes used for what has no connection to experience or concrete things, as if it were an arbitrary invention, but abstract (Lat.: *ab*, "from," + *trahere*, "to draw") means a concept which has been drawn forth from particulars and experience.

Without abstractions we could not live through the day.

intension, see "intention"

intention, intension, extension

"Intention" means the purpose one has in mind, but "intension"

(spelled with a difference) in logic means all the properties sig-
nified by a term: its connotations.

"Extension" means the scope or extent of something. It may be
a primary quality of things, for things are extended in space. In
logic "extension" (without change of spelling) means the things
denoted by a term.

With good intention you should be able to keep these words
clear. In logic: extension = the totality of objects denoted by a
term; intension = the defining characteristics of a term.

intermediate, see "immediate"

intersubjectivity, see "subject"

intuition

In common usage "intuition" means lucky guesswork, popularly
reserved for women in general or specific horseplayers. In philosophy "intuition" means immediate or direct knowledge. It may play
an important role in scientific knowledge as well as in morality and
religious experience. Problem: How does one know what intuition
is? Answer: Intuitively. Intuition also has a broader sense in philosophy as that which strikes one as right before or independently
of thorough inquiry. Philosophers then try to work out sound
theories which will be in conformity with such intuitions (see
"prescientific"). (For further discussion of the place of intuition in
philosophic reasoning see ch. 4.)

Logical Positivism, see "Positivism"

Materialism, see "materialist"

materialist, Materialism

A materialist in popular terms is someone attached to money and
possessions, but in philosophy he is someone, like Lucretius, who
adheres to the theory that matter is the underlying substance of
things, including what we call mental activity. (See "epiphenomenalism.") Materialism is opposed to Idealism. (See "Dialectical
Materialism.")

mean, means, meaning, golden mean, ends-means continuum

The mean is a quantitative notion of a balancing point or intermediary between points. The means is the instrumentation for arriv-
ing at some point. Thus, the mean stands in relation to the ex-
tremes, while the means stands in relation to the end.

Aristotle argues that virtue is the mean between the excess and
deficiency which are vices (*Nicomachean Ethics*, Bk. II, chs. 6–8,
1106^a–1109^b). This is sometimes referred to as the "golden mean."

Dewey argues that a means to an end can become valued as an
end itself, just as an end can serve as a means to another end.
[John Dewey, *Theory of Valuation*, Vol. II, No. 4 of the *International Encyclopedia of Unified Science* (Chicago: University of Chicago
Press, 1962), ch. 6, pp. 40–50.] This is known as the "ends-means
continuum."

I trust you now know what "mean" can mean and what "means" means. The meaning of "meaning" itself is subject to study in philosophy. The meaning of words is studied by the linguistic science of semantics.

meaning, see "mean"

means, see "mean"

mediate, see "immediate"

meta-

The first "meta" discipline we have in philosophy is metaphysics, so named by the early editor of Aristotle who placed his books on "First Philosophy" after (Gr.: *meta*) his *Physics*. John of Salisbury wrote a *Metalogicon* and Freud wrote essays in metapsychology. The philosophic fashion now includes metaethics, metalanguage, metascience, and even a journal of *Metaphilosophy*. We are far from reaching a met*ameta* period. Roughly speaking, the use of the prefix "meta" signifies a field of fundamental principles upon which an ordinary field of knowledge rests, or else the meta field is one in which the very field it is meta to is discussed.

metaphysical, see "mystical"

moment

A "moment" generally refers to an unmeasurable unit of time, but there is an additional philosophic sense which is not temporal: moment can be the constituent element of the analysis of something.

monism, see "dualism"

more geometrico

Lat.: "in the geometrical manner," that is, a deductive (see "deduction") sequence of propositions similar to the presentation of Euclid. Spinoza uses this method for his *Ethics*.

mysterious, see "mystical"

mystical, mythical, metaphysical, mysterious

These words are easily mixed up because of their similarity of sound and the fact that they may all refer to divine matters. They are not equivalent. The mystical is direct knowledge without reason (see "intuition," "immediate"); the mysterious is puzzling or intellectually unclear; the metaphysical (see "meta-") is fundamentally real or essential; the mythical is legendary or imaginary. Mysticism does indeed pose mysteries for most metaphysicians. In satirical usage or that of Logical Positivism, "metaphysical" is a term of scorn meaning learned nonsense. (On metaphysics as a branch of philosophy see ch. 2.)

mythical, see "mystical"

necessary and sufficient condition, contingent condition

A necessary condition for something is one without which it could not possibly occur, e.g. a person has to be alive in order to have the right to vote (graveyard ballots are illegal). But having the necessary condition for something does not mean that you thereby have it, as being alive does not guarantee you the vote (citizenship is also required).

A sufficient condition is one that suffices, i. e. is itself enough, to bring about something in question. When the sufficient condition is present, it must occur. The sufficient condition therefore is the sum of all necessary conditions.

We generally proceed by identifying one by one the necessary conditions, which are not sufficient until we arrive at that condition which is necessary *and* sufficient. It is necessary for you to have a sufficient grasp of such logical criteria.

Necessary as a condition may also be distinguished from the contingent: A necessary condition must be present for something to occur; it is essential. A contingent condition is not a necessary one; it may be present but need not be for something to be brought about (see "accidental"). The discussion of all these conditions occurs in the analysis of causality and in the logic of implication.

nothing, see "being"

noumenal, see "phenomenon"

null set, see "being"

object, see "subject"

paradox, see "dilemma"

passion, action

In ordinary usage doing something passionately can mean putting much action into it. In philosophy there is a narrower sense of passion which puts it in opposition to action. You undergo or suffer a passion when forces beyond your control act upon you, but when you act it is you who control your deeds (see "praxis," "will"). Passions may interfere with one's reasoning as well as with one's actions. Spinoza wrote of the passions or emotions under the title "Of Human Bondage" (*Ethics*, Pt. IV). (See *amor intellectualis Dei.*)

penultimate, see "ultimate"

percept, precept

A percept is something perceived; a precept is a rule. Make it a rule to perceive the difference between these two terms. (See *esse est percipi.*)

Phenomenology, see "phenomenon"

phenomenon, noumenal, Phenomenology, epiphenomenalism

"Phenomenon" is a term appearing frequently in scientific writings. It is a Greek participle meaning "appearing." "Phenomenon" is singular; its plural is "phenomena." A phenomenon is an appearance, an observable, a happening; it is not necessarily an entity, a fact, or a reality. Science aims to explain phenomena, to identify their causes, and to predict their occurrence.

Something "phenomenal," like a racing car, is in popular terms a marvel, but something "phenomenal" in philosophy refers to experience that appears to the awareness. The phenomenal is contrasted with the noumenal, which is its supposed ground but is not knowable in experience (see *Ding-an-sich*).

Epiphenomenalism is the theory that the mind is merely a derivative occurrence or phenomenon of the material brain (see "Materialism").

Phenomenology as founded by Edmund Husserl is a rigorous introspective method of examining the phenomena of the mind in its own activity of thought.

philosophes, see "philosophizing"

philosophizing, doing philosophy, being philosophical, *philosophes*

The correct verb for the conduct of philosophy is "philosophizing" and it has been used throughout this book. But many philosophers shy away from using that verb to apply to their activity because of its popular connotations: to philosophize may mean to make pompous and grave pronouncements. Similarly, "being philosophical," instead of simply meaning the conduct of oneself in accordance with philosophic understanding, can be construed as being sententious, maudlin, and otherwise affected. "To take things like a philosopher" is an idiomatic expression meaning to withstand adversity like a Stoic. Some instructors and writers may speak of "doing philosophy" in place of these expressions with their distorting associations.

In the eighteenth century "philosophy" had a broader meaning as organized knowledge, proper method, and progressive conduct; thus the *philosophes* in France, such as Voltaire and Diderot, were enlightened thinkers whatever the field of inquiry or practice.

Positivism, Logical Positivism

A positive or positivistic approach to philosophy means seeking after claims that have practical application or else empirically verifiable contents, instead of speculative or metaphysical conclusions. Positivism is a nineteenth-century movement led by Auguste Comte with strong emphasis on applied science. Logical Positivism is a twentieth-century movement, also scientific, but with greater emphasis on the logic and language of science. Logical Positivists, such as Rudolf Carnap and Alfred Jules Ayer, have rejected metaphysics as verbiage without meaning.

potential, see "actual"

pragmatic, Pragmatism, praxis

In ordinary usage the "pragmatic" has come to mean something which is practical or useful, but that is too simple a sense for philosophy. Something pragmatic, as stipulated by Pragmatists such as Charles S. Peirce and William James, may gain its *meaning* by reference to the consequences of actions.

"Praxis" is a handy Greek word that philosophers apply to action, doing, or practice. Its antonyms may be "passion" or "theory." Dialectical Materialism claims to be a science of praxis.

Pragmatism, see "pragmatic"

praxis, see "pragmatic"

precept, see "percept"

predetermination, see "determinism"

predicate term, see "proposition"

prescientific

Ordinarily, "prescientific" refers to that stage in the history of civilization before the rise of scientific thinking, but in recent philosophic examinations of language, logic, and science, "prescientific" means statements that are not rigorously formulated within the system. Such statements are made off the cuff, but that doesn't mean they are incapable of correct, "scientific," formulation. (See "intuition.")

primary and secondary qualities

Philosophers may discuss the qualities of things, of sensations, or of things-as-sensed. Some division is usually made between primary (such as size, shape, extension) and secondary (such as color, taste, odor, sound). Two questions for you to determine are where a philosopher draws the line between the primary and secondary, and exactly what he takes them to be qualities of. (See *Ding-an-sich*, "phenomenon," "sensible," "subject.")

principal, see "principle"

principle, principal

"Principle" and "principal," which are pronounced identically and spring from the same root (Lat: *princip*, "first"), are confounded daily. They are both valuable words with some overlap of meaning. Keep in mind the primary sense in which they differ. Philosophy aims at and builds from principles, which are the rules or foundations of a discipline or subject matter. A principal thing is a chief or main thing. The *principle*, then, is a starting point, while the *principal* is the main point. In principle philosophy seeks and builds from principles, and principally it does arrive at what is principal. There are different kinds and sources of principles (see *a priori, cogito ergo sum*, "conscience," *esse est percipi*, "Existentialism," "idea," "initial," "principle of indeterminancy"). (For discussion of the place of principles in philosophic reasoning see ch. 4.)

principle of indeterminancy, see "indeterminism"

proposition, analytic proposition, synthetic proposition, predicate term

A "proposition" commonly is used in the sense of an offer, deal, or proposal. In philosophy a proposition is a claim, statement, or assertion which is either true or false. The proposition is the unit of argument. Its status in logic is comparable to that of the sentence in grammar. Propositions are classified as to their quality (affirmative or negative) and quantity (universal or particular). "All men and women are mortal" is a universal affirmative proposition. Its logical parts can be identified in this way: "all" is the *quantifier*, "men and women" is the *subject term*, "are" is the *copula*, and "mortal" is the *predicate term*, or what is being attributed via the copula to the subject term in the quantity designated.

You are likely to find mention in philosophy of analytic and synthetic propositions. The truth of an analytic proposition is determined from within itself due to its very wording, e.g., "An apple is a fruit." The truth of a synthetic proposition requires reference outside of itself to other propositions or sources, e.g., "There are apples on the tree." Problem: Is the analytic-synthetic distinction an analytic or synthetic distinction? Analytic propositions and *a priori* knowledge are often taken to be the same. Kant is an important exception, as he makes a case for something that is a synthetic *a priori* proposition.

(See "categorical," "contradictory," "deduction," "implication," "paradox," "tautology," "thesis.")

proximate cause, see "cause"

raison d'être, see "rationalize"

randomness, see "indeterminism"

rationale, see "rationalize"

Rationalism, see "rationalize"

rationalize, reasoning, being rational, Rationalism, rationale, *raison d'être*

"To rationalize" means to offer excuses which only have the appearance of being justifying reasons. Hence, rationalizing does not belong in philosophy. Being rational and conducting one's discourse rationally are desirable since they mean reasoning, the offering of reasons. "Rationale" (from the Latin) and *raison d'être* (from the French) are other ways of referring to the reason for something. (See "absurdity," "dialectic," "dilemma" and "paradox," "induction" and "deduction," "passion," "philosophizing," "thesis" and related words.)

Rationalists in philosophy (such as Descartes) hold that the sign of truth is discoverable in the mind and that it is by connecting ideas (usually by deduction) that we advance knowledge. Their theory is called "Rationalism" and is opposed to Empiricism. But Rationalists are not to be mistaken for rationalizers; nor do you have to be a Rationalist to discourse rationally.

realize

Ordinarily, "to realize" something means to become aware of it (see "conscious"). In philosophy "to realize" may have a literal sense of to make real, as in "History realizes the Idea of Freedom in Nature" (Hegel). Ambiguity can be avoided by utilizing "recognize" for being aware, and reserving "realize" for making real. (See "actual" and "potential.")

reasoning, see "rationalize"
reductio ad absurdum, see "absurdity"
self-contradiction, see "dilemma"
semantical, see "semantics"
semantics, semantical, syntactical
> The popular phrase "that's just semantics" means quibbling over
> words. That is unfortunate because it debases the meaning of
> "semantics." There is a linguistic science of semantics which deals
> with the meanings of words. In philosophy of language and logic,
> the "semantical" refers to the meaning or content of claims, and is
> distinguished from the "syntactical" or purely formal attributes of
> claims. (See "meaning," "proposition.")
sensation, see "sensible"
sensible, sensual, sensation
> There are some sharp differences in philosophic usage from the or-
> dinary senses of these related words. In theory of knowledge the
> "sensible" generally means capable of being sensed rather than rea-
> sonable; the "sensual" generally means imbued with the sensory
> rather than voluptuous; and the "sensational" generally means re-
> lated to sensations rather than shocking. Does that make sense?
> Now explain what a "sensible object" (Berkeley) is in epis-
> temological terms. (See "primary and secondary qualities.")
sensual, see "sensible"
solipsism
> Solipsism is the predicament of being limited in one's knowledge
> to that which occurs in one's experience or thinking. Hume man-
> ages to philosophize from within this predicament. Solipsism be-
> comes a fallacy when it is claimed that nothing exists except what
> is within one's experience or that it is one's experience that makes
> things exist.
soul
> In popular usage "soul" refers to the spiritual being of man, his
> eternal and holy self as distinct from his mere mind. The term is
> used with much greater latitude of meaning in philosophy. It can
> mean the mind, the spirit, the self, the mental life, and the psychic
> functions generally, including appetite, desire, reason, and imagi-
> nation (cf. Aristotle). A philosophic mention of the soul does not
> imply a commitment to immortality or divinity. Philosophers may
> speak of the soul of something, whether it be tragedy or the uni-
> verse, in the sense of its governing principle. The Greek word is
> *psyche* (from whence "psychology," the science of . . . ?), the Latin
> *anima*, the French is the related *âme*, and the German is *Seele*, a
> cousin to our "soul." (See "conscious" and related terms, "epiphe-
> nomenalism," "feeling," "passion," "reasoning.")
subconscious, see "conscious"
subject, object, intersubjectivity, subject term
> "Subject" and "object" are valuable terms in ordinary speech, in

grammar, and in psychology, as well as in logic, theory of knowledge, and Existentialism. In general philosophic usage the subject is the person, the one who experiences, the perceiver, knower, or agent, while the object is a thing, that which is perceived, known, or acted upon, "Subjective" as an adjective refers to the conditions of the subject; "objective" refers to the conditions of the thing itself.

Note that in ordinary speech "subjective" applied to an account may be pejorative, indicating that it is unrealistic or unsubstantiated, while in philosophy subjective accounts may be founded on real experience since the subject itself is real. Thus, Husserl founded Phenomenology as an exact science of pure subjectivity. Existentialism also takes its stand within subjectivity and explores the problems of intersubjectivity, that is, the connections between people.

An objective account ordinarily means a truthful, dispassionate one, even if it is describing a person's experience. In philosophy "objective" may have the narrower sense of merely referring to things, the objects of knowledge. The "object" may also be used in the sense of purpose (see "end") and refer to persons, as in: "The object of the constitution is the safety of the people."

Once you keep the subject/object distinction clear you will find that philosophy poses new and fascinating problems involving them. Thus, since the object is known only by the subject, can the object ever be known as itself (see *Ding-an-sich*) or are we condemned to perpetual subjective reports (see "solipsism") about it? Is size an objective quality of a thing or a subjective quality of a viewer (see "phenomenon" and "noumenal," "primary and secondary qualities")? How do I know that other people are subjects like myself and not mere objects of nature like trees?

In logic the subject term of a proposition is that about which the proposition makes its claim, as in "Socrates is mortal" mortality is attributed to (predicated of) the subject Socrates. "Mortal" is the predicate term. There is no object term in logic. Note that the subject term need not be limited to a single word and like the subject in grammar need not come at the beginning of the sentence. In "Happy is she who has used her mind well," the subject term is "she who has used her mind well." Problem: What is the predicate term in the proposition?

subject term, see "subject"

sub specie æternitatas

Lat.: viewed in the light of eternity. Often said of God's outlook upon things (Spinoza). (See "eternal.")

summum bonum

Lat.: "the supreme good."

syntactical, see "semantics"

synthesis, see "thesis"

synthetic proposition, see "proposition"

tautology

A tautology (Gr.: *tauto* + *logia*, "same words," "double-talk") is a statement that merely repeats what it is saying in a different way: "A bachelor is an unmarried man." "A mind is a thing which thinks" (Descartes). Ordinarily, tautologies are to be avoided as not saying anything new; they are trivial and redundant. A tautology in logic is a propositional form which must always be true due to its form, such as "*A* or not *A*," an instance of which is, "It is raining or it is not raining." Problems in logic can be resolved by reducing or transforming propositions by means of rules which are tautologous. (See "analytic proposition.")

teleology, see "end"

theocracy, see "theology"

theodicy, see "theology"

theology, theodicy, theocracy

A number of interesting words are built upon the Greek prefix *theos*, meaning "god." Theology is the study of God. It may be applied to theories within philosophy concerning divinity, but it is more applicable to a discipline outside of philosophy which works out the consequences of certain religious commitments (see philosophy of religion as a branch of philosophy, in ch. 2).

Theodicy is the attempt to justify (Gr.: *dike*, "justice") the existence of evil in God's world (see "fatalism"). The term was coined by Leibniz.

A theocracy is a form of government under God or a priesthood. There is no separation of Church and State in a theocracy

thesis, antithesis, synthesis, hypothesis

A thesis is a setting forth, a stand taken up, a position (a position is not a posture). When a thesis is advanced it must be argued for. A thesis is not merely a theme or a topic. An antithesis is a counterclaim. The opposition of two theses is also called an "antithesis." A synthesis is a conjoining. To synthesize is to bring together what may be disparate or in opposition. In dialectical reasoning (see "dialectic") the synthesis comprehends thesis and its antithesis and goes beyond them. The synthesis works out the grain of truth embedded in both thesis and antithesis and causes it to sprout into something new. An Hegelian example of this process in history: first one was free (the Oriental despot), but this was opposed when some were free (the Greek citizens), and finally this gives rise to all being free (the contribution of the German nation aided by Christianity).

An hypothesis is a working position, a stand taken up experimentally for the sake of argument or inquiry. It is subject to correction, rejection, or verification in its very utilization. An hypothesis is a trial proposition or tentative principle. Etymologically, the word means setting a foundation in place.

A "hypothetical proposition" is a technical name for what is also called an "implication."

transcendental, see "immanent"

ultimate, initial, penultimate

The ultimate is last. It is the final stage in a series. It may be the most important or the superlative stage or item, as is reflected in the idiomatic, "that's the ultimate in such-and-such!" The initial is first. It is sometimes said in philosophy, "God is the ultimate cause of the universe," instead of "God is the first (or initial) cause." The explanation for this is that although God may be first in the chain of causality, He or She is last in the regressive chain of analysis whereby we seek out the starting point. In the last analysis, God is first. God may also be said to be the ultimate cause as the greatest of the causes involved. There is some trickiness, then, in the philosophic usage of these words, but ultimately you will have to keep beginnings clear from ends, and it is wise to do so initially.

The last of a chain of causes immediately preceding something is called the "proximate cause." Penultimate is next to last. Intermediate is somewhere between initial and ultimate (see "mean").

uncertainty principle, see "indeterminism"

unconscious, see "conscious"

Weltanschauung

Ger.: "outlook on the world," the set of attitudes or the personal "philosophy" one has on life, distinguished from a reasoned philosophical position. Some thinkers, such as Freud and Karl Mannheim, see a person's *Weltanschauung* as more important and authentic than a person's philosophical theories. (See "intuition," *philosophes*, "prescientific.")

will, free will

In general usage a "will" is a legal document and "will" is an auxiliary verb noting futurity, e.g. "I will do it tomorrow." In philosophical discourse the will (often capitalized) is the decision-making power or faculty of a person. It is the locus of deliberation and choice. The verb "willing" indicates a voluntary act, e.g. "I will to do it tomorrow." "Free will" refers to the independence of the will from total determinism by natural events. The free will is a cause in the world without being the mere effect of motives or outside forces (see "indeterminism"). For a number of philosophers, including Schopenhauer and Nietzsche, the will is a force stronger than reason, largely unconscious, and a vital drive toward realization (see "realize"). It is as if where there is a way there is a will. Be willing to detect these ways of speaking. (See "action," "cause," "teleology.")

6

Writing Philosophically

Writing as learning. Students often think that the sole purpose of written assignments in college is the exhibition of their knowledge for the sake of being graded. That is not accurate. Writing is a dimension of the learning experience in your courses, especially in philosophy. It presents you with the challenge of organizing your ideas, putting them into words in a fashion that is true to your insight, and getting them down on paper so that they can be critically examined by yourself and others. In meeting this challenge, you discover—not simply express—what you think. You will find that what you think you thought when you didn't have to write it differs from what you see you think when you set it out before you. Before you wrote you thought you knew; after writing you know what you thought. *See what you think: write philosophy.*

It is easy for the mind to deceive itself, telling itself that it has the answer to some problem. In writing you have to work out the answers. You discover difficulties in matching your understanding with effective words. This may very well be because you don't understand something as clearly as you thought you did. Writing is a way of thinking, not merely a report of what has been thought.

Writing not only gives you the chance to work out your ideas; it is also a valuable opportunity for self-criticism, because you have to read what you have written with a critical eye. Thus, writing is a method of introspection whereby you can correct what you find in your own thought. It allows you to see your own philosophical activity much as you can see and assess the workings of philosophy in the texts you read by others.

Finally, writing affords a deeper insight into the problems of argument and communication faced by other writers, including those you have read. You will be fairer to them once you have tried your hand at it yourself.

Writing, then, is an integral part of your development as a thinker, yet the art of writing is being swamped by the high tide of illiteracy. Hence, considerable space must be given the subject in this philosophical handbook.

The problem.   In dealing with the task of writing an essay or term paper your first concern should be with the *problem* involved. Sometimes you will be assigned the problem, but more often the general topic will be given under which many problems may be located. Frequently students are asked to choose a topic of their own, as long as it is related to the course, and to work on a worthwhile problem under that topic. Even when the problem is given you, there may well be a number of issues that constitute it, or a number of ways of reshaping the whole problem so that again you have a choice of what to concentrate upon.

In any case, *you are responsible for the problem you deal with.* This means you must be aware of what is problematic about it. You ought to have some sense of alternative approaches to the issue at stake. Selecting a problem requires a weighing process of selection. You must work out the best resolution you can, while being honest about its shortcomings and about the advantages of other resolutions.

Before you begin writing make sure you have a philosophical problem. If you don't you are going to have other problems. A philosophical problem is not simply a subject matter, like "free will," on which you say whatever you think. It should be some disputable issue which you concentrate on clarifying and resolving, such as the conflict between the free choice made by the soul and the physical determinism of the body. A great deal of thought must go into defining the problem and working it out. Perhaps half the job of writing philosophy consists in isolating the problem and probing it with thoroughness before you set a word on paper.

Finding a problem. Where do you start *in finding your problem?* Begin with the assignment made by the instructor. See if it poses any limits as to what you should treat or if it recommends topics to be explored. This can circumscribe or guide your consideration.

The easiest way to get a problem for your paper is to simply take one of those discussed in the course. For this very reason instructors often preclude such a choice. After all, you are expected to be able to do a thorough job on the assigned materials in class and on examinations. Therefore, the essay you write should be an occasion to see what you can do on fresh materials of your own selection. You may find such materials for thought in some issue touched on only tangentially in class or in the readings. Think back over your discussions, look through your notes, glance over your annotated readings. You may find a problem that caught your interest at the time but had to be left untreated as the arguments advanced.

A good source for philosophic problems, is, of course, philosophical texts. Do some more reading. You may find stimulating approaches to fresh problems that set you thinking on the problems yourself. If an author in the course has particularly interested you, why not read another of his works? If you are using a book of readings, you can read a few unassigned selections which will improve your understanding of problems and areas that were assigned as well as open new issues. But you may be disappointed by any of these readings; you may find nothing that stimulates you to write first-hand and you may not wish to critically evaluate the author's work. Indeed, you may have trouble understanding the reading, which only makes more problems for you in your search for a problem. Therefore, give yourself ample time to read exploratively and to discard what is of no help. (See ch. 3 on reading.)

It is not necessary to read in order to find problems. You can think them up yourself. And you may have a solution in mind to some issue barely mentioned in the course. An essay is a good opportunity for working out as completely as you can some of the insights, questions, and arguments you have had in mind. You may also want to start completely afresh with some subject you have not given much serious thought to. Exploring it in thought can open up interesting difficulties, argumentative leads, and some alternatives for choice.

Narrowing the problem. Once you have your problem, or more likely an area of related problems, cut it down to *something manageable.* In order to do an adequate job of critical evaluation it is best to select a salient issue within the major problem. For instance, you may be interested in the nature and existence of God. You might then direct your attention to proofs of His or Her existence. There are quite a number of plausible and controversial proofs made available by philosophers. As you think over the proofs, or as you read some of them, your interest might light on some one particular line of argument, say the proof through regress of causal chains. This will lead you to think about the concept of causality. There are many implications for the empirical sciences in such a concept. Soon you will have encountered quite a number of questions concerning God, human knowledge, scientific theory, and the structure of the physical world. For your paper select one of these areas. It might be the necessity of empirical science to assume a first cause (God) in order that knowledge may be had of the universe. Or it might be the logical status of causality itself. Your paper might turn out to be on an epistemological or logical problem rather than on the ontological problem of God. (Can you distinguish these three kinds of philosophical problems? See ch. 2.)

Even given one of these topics you may narrow it down further, directing your scrutiny to just a few points touching the issue. The more you limit the scope of the problem you treat, the more thoroughly you will be able to treat it. The process of narrowing the topic into a problem is a process of coming to understand what the problem is. By coming to it in this reflective manner you are ready to work on its resolution. Thus, you don't simply start with the problem; you arrive at it. Difficulties are compounded when papers take on too big a topic, such as the meaning of life, the structure of the universe, and the direction of history. Such papers are forced to remain at a level of generality which does not get down to disputed issues, contending alternatives, and concrete insights. That is, they keep one from exercising precise philosophic analysis and resolution of problematic matters. The danger in generality is the temptation to resort to platitude and pomposity. A major fault in many beginning papers is that they lack a clear sense of the problematic. They may be *about* some topic but they do not go about probing it as a difficulty.

You may have acquired good habits of selection in your reading, discussions, and lectures, but the task of writing requires even narrower selection of problems. It takes more time to put things down on paper, and you will have to do a much closer job in writing your arguments than you do in the midst of discussion. Make sure, then, that you have a manageable problem for the time and effort that will be available.

Term paper.   *Term paper* is a technical term in college for the major essay written during a course and submitted toward the end of the term. Yet it is a misnomer, since you do not have the entire term to work on it. Some students regard a term paper as an assignment that can be put off for most of the term. Others treat it as a task that can be attended to at any date in the course and that has no intimate connection to the coursework. Your term paper may well have to be submitted long before the end of the term, and it will probably be several weeks before you are ready to start work on it. Even in the remaining middle part of the term you will have to keep up with your classwork, which can include other written work such as exams. What you are learning from the coursework may change your mind about the term paper; it may even cause you to abandon the problem you planned to work on. Hence, it is best to face this truth: you have rather limited time in which to do a term paper.

Time. You will need time to think about what your paper is to be about. Once you have decided on the problem you will have to think about it. You may do some reading on the subject. You will need time to be at a loss, to be thrown off the track, and even to abandon the problem if it is not proving fruitful. When you have found something that is working out in your thinking you will need the time to put it into writing. Writing is not as easy as you think, for writing is your thinking on difficult matters. There should be time to toss your writing aside and come back to it, time to tear it up and start over. When your paper is written you must have time to read it. And after reading it, your job is to re-read it. Time to revise, to perfect, and even to rewrite is quite important. Then you can hand it in.

Length. There is a *length limit* on your paper. It may be one specified by the instructor, but there is also a limit on what you can write in the time you have and with the other work you are responsible for. If you set to work on a problem that requires one hundred pages of discussion, then it is fair to say that you have picked something too big. And if you can treat the subject in one page, then the problem is too small. What is the proper length of a term paper? Somewhere between one and one hundred pages. If there is no prescribed limit, calculate (1) what length of treatment the problem demands, and (2) what you can accomplish in the limited time. You will have to adjust these calculations to one another and revise both as you proceed. It will take several terms of college work for you to judge fairly accurately in advance what length a prospective paper will be. Yet the length of a philosophy paper is only known when you finish it. Each paper dictates its own length in terms of the nature of the problem, the materials used, the nature of the resolution, the time available to develop particular points, and the writing style of the individual.

Essay. A term paper as a *philosophic essay* is an original exploration of a problem by inquiry and argument, aiming at the critical resolution of what is at issue in the best way possible. The philosophic essay is a microcosm of philosophical work as a whole. An essay is not a report, not a confession, not a set of pronouncements, but an active tangling with difficulties in the effort to disentangle them. The essay is a *try-*

ing. The word is from the French verb *essayer*, "to try or make an effort," and the modern essay took its place as an intellectual activity with the *Essais* of Montaigne (1580). One of the peculiarities of the philosophic essay is that once it begins one cannot be sure where it will end. *An essay is an activity of exploration.* It involves struggle along the way because it is an encounter with the problematic. If there is no problem, hence no struggle, there is nothing to be discovered and there is no need for an essay. If all the discoveries have been made and no problems remain, then one writes a treatise rather than an essay. Of course, there are treatises in philosophy. You have probably read some, and you might even be ready to write one. Sometimes a paper is assigned in the history of philosophy in which you are primarily *to report* on how a problem was covered or resolved by another thinker. But it is the original essay that many instructors will require of you whether it be a brief one or a term paper, and whether you are to deal with contributions by others or not.

In your essay do not merely sum up class discussion. This you should be able to do without writing a paper. Your essay is an occasion to go beyond discussion or lectures in your original pursuit of problems. If you write something that could be written without taking the course, you are missing something, namely the course. Your writing in the course should show what you have been gaining from the experience. That doesn't mean repeating the material studied or projecting "what the instructor wants," but it does mean putting to use the expanded understanding which you have been developing.

Intellectual contents. What should be in your philosophical essay? First of all, *exposition* appropriate to the problem and to the contributions of any authors used. Your job is to make clear what is at issue, why it is important, how it comes to be problematic, and what can be done about it. Don't proceed immediately to resolve the problem or to criticize false resolutions. Build the problem for the reader, set it up in your own words so that he can appreciate your criticism and understand your proposed resolution. Don't assume that the reader knows what you are talking about when you mention an issue: make the reader *see* what the issue is.

If you are using the works of other philosophers as springboards for your discussion be sure to give them a fair representation. Indicate what their positions are before you approve or disapprove. Don't assume that the reader of your essay is familiar with the writers you have consulted or understands them in the way you do. When presenting the work of others you should analyze their arguments—that is, expose the structure of their reasoning—and, if you wish, you may reformulate their arguments in your own terms, making use of your own insights.

Avoid summarizing, condensing, paraphrasing, quoting extensively, or otherwise repeating what your author has said. These procedures merely give evidence that you have read the words in the text. They do not show that you have understood what you have read. The reader of your essay could just as well read the author you deal with. The trouble with many a philosophic essay on an author is that it is only on the author—that is, it doesn't get down to the problems faced by the author that are to be dealt with by the essay writer. Don't let your author do your paper in place of you. In writing philosophy you are the primary author.

In addition to clarification and analysis of any writings you use, you should employ *critical evaluation*. Show precisely where your author is right or wrong and why. And as you deal with other arguments that may not come from material read, they too must be subjected to assessment. Don't make your job too easy by dealing only with obviously weak approaches. Spend your time on the best approaches you can find and then try to closely weigh their exact worth.

A *critical comparison* of two positions does not consist of stating first one position and then the other, concluding with a sentence pronouncing one or the other to be right. *To critically compare is to bring into confrontation positions that conflict.* Show point by point their disagreements and weigh the merits as you proceed. Your judgment should not merely be presented at the end but should be exercised throughout the comparison. Allow the positions to challenge one another, to urge their alternatives, to open up the issues so that you may intercede. In a critical comparison of two positions there is always a third position present, yours, which must make its criteria evident and support its judgment.

As a culmination of critical weighing of positions, your paper should include your best effort at a *resolution*. Make a stand. Put yourself into the discussion. Take hold of the problem. In making a stand you are responsible for supporting it. Argue for your views, don't just state them. Serve the truth by its advocacy. But while you make a case for your resolution, show awareness of the pertinent objections to be raised against it and of the merits still residing in rejected cases.

As you write your term paper or long essay you may feel the urge toward *theory construction*, not content to settle one problem but thirsting to go forward with your method and insight to set straight half a dozen related problems. There are risks in following the urge. If you have the time and paper more power to you. But if you can't get a full job done on it, then it is likely to turn out to be superficial. Instead of the comprehensive resolution that goes to the depths of a subject area, you might be handing in a sketchy survey. To do a whole theory is mightily ambitious. It is prudent to at least work out with thoroughness one distinct problem before you continue writing your larger plans. Take the time to think in large theoretical terms while engaged in the paper, even if there is no place for them in the writing of it (see thinking theoretically, ch. 4).

Formal writing.   Writing assignments in college are occasions for *formal writing*. They require a care for composition, style, and correctness of language which you are not accustomed to in sending a postcard, writing a letter home, keeping a diary, jotting down notes, or leaving a telephone message. Formal writing must be well organized, not scattered; complete in its expression, not fragmentary; correct in its structure, not capricious. Formal writing is not a private notation for only you and your friends to read, but is intended for the objective examination of a disinterested party. There are some common aspects of speech or informal writing that do not belong in formal writing: "Get what I mean?" And there are some useful aspects of formal writing that do not generally occur in other writing or speech, such as the scholarly use of Latin abbreviations (see below).

Formal writing is not to be confounded with formal dress: it should not be stiff and aristocratic. You may feel uncomfortable in writing formally because it seems artificial and distant from your personal style of expression. Yes, good writing intended for dispassionate study by others is artificial because it must be constructed. You have to work at expressing yourself clearly in other than a personal way. Yet what you do come to express is yourself. You can better see what you think when you have done your thinking in formal writing.

Above all, formal writing is important to your work in philosophy. Since philosophic discourse deals with arguments and explores reasons concerning disputed problems, it must be clear and grammatically correct in its statements, it must be carefully organized in its written presentation, and it must be communicated in a dispassionate and plain language accessible to the understanding of the general reader. Virtually all of philosophic writing intended for publication has been written formally.

I hear you protest: "So you philosophers are holding my poor writing against me as if this were an English course!" But a philosophy course is an English course insofar as it is conducted in English, for standards of intelligibility and correctness apply to the use of language. If your poor English makes your work in philosophy suffer, then you had best work intensively on the improvement of your English. Philosophy cannot give you a dispensation from clarity, intelligibility, and correctness in language.

You should be prepared not only to overcome all difficulties of style and expression in the writings of others but to eliminate all such difficulties from your own writing. If a point is worth making it is worth making well, that means with clarity and correctness of statement. Take good care of your writing, for it is a part of your intellectual life that you might be proud of. Set high standards and see that every syllable conforms to them. It may take years for you to reach those standards but it is better to move in the right direction than to leave untried one's capabilities.

"True ease in writing comes from art, not chance." [Alexander Pope, "An Essay on Criticism," Pt. II, verse 362.] The art of philosophic writing requires us not to make the mistakes evident in what already has been written, even by ourselves. To write philosophically is to have learned from writings and to learn from writing. Get it right.

The reader is human and must read other essays. Make his job easier by being straightforward. You may have struggled to make sense out of your topic, but that is no reason why the reader should be made to struggle to make sense out of your paper. I have heard this defense from students: "I thought you would understand what I meant, so I didn't explain it." Don't be so trusting in the understanding of your instructors. Take the trouble to explain what you mean so that it is understandable. Make your words our words.

Avoid introduction, apology, repeating the assignment, repeating your statements, long quotations, excessive examples, digressions, personal confessions, and summary. Whatever is left, if anything, is the heart of the philosophic writing: build it into the entire essay.

An essay is not one paragraph. A paragraph is not one sentence. A sentence is not a pile of words. A word is not an idea. An essay is an organization of points in paragraphs each of which develops one line of thought by means of sentences which are complete units of thought making correct use of words which properly conjoined are able to express ideas. Got it? Do it. Your writing should serve your thinking, not swerve it. Your thoughts must not simply flow; they must follow from each other.

Use examples of your own invention at crucial points, but use them in moderation. Each example you use should be exploited for maximum comprehension by making clear (1) what it is supposed to exemplify, (2) how it does exemplify, and (3) what result follows from the fact that it does exemplify some point. Announcing something as an example does not make it one. (On the proper use of examples see ch. 4.)

Do not attack persons. Concern yourself with arguments. You don't have to denounce arguments and fulminate against them if they are fallacious; just show them to be fallacious. In philosophy—though not in the history of philosophy—it is totally irrelevant who advanced an argument, when, in what country or classroom, or for what personal motive.

In philosophic writing let the arguments speak for themselves. Argue by presenting your reasons; don't apologize by offering your feelings. Don't couch your claims in personal language, such as "I feel that . . . ." If nothing can be said for your views other than that they are your opinions, then you might be better off without those opinions. Think them over and decide upon your commitments. Put on paper what you are ready to argue for.

Putting words down.   Be precise, be concise, be incisive. Write simply. Get to the point and stick to the point. Above all be clear. Do not adopt a flowery style. You are not writing poetry. Do not regress to primitive structure. An essay is not a telegram. Put ideas into the clearest language of twentieth-century English that can be understood by an ordinary reader. Take time to explain. A carefully and fully explained point is worth half a dozen hastily established points that subsequently you may have to abandon. If you have trouble starting start anyway. Then, once you are on your way, you can return to the false start and delete it or adjust it to fit where you are going.

Don't deal with things "on first impression," "at first glance," but present your most mature reflection on the subject. A colleague tells me that when she reads the sentence, "The first thing that came into my mind . . .," the first thing that comes into her mind is that the author will reject what he is about to report, hence the reader might as well save time by skipping ahead to something more substantial.

Avoid noncommittal phrases, such as "perhaps she is right," "I don't know the answer but my position is . . . ," "I feel this is wrong." Be assertive. Show that an argument is right or wrong, or else indicate the specific doubts you have about it. If your assertiveness cannot be firm, be firm in indicating why not. If your firmness cannot be assertive, then be assertive in indicating why not. What this means is (1) you must take a stand in philosophy, and (2) any stand taken must be reasoned for. To not take a stand is also to take a stand and requires justification.

Don't use the language of feelings when what is called for is the language of reason. In place of "I feel" use "I contend," "I assert," "I argue," "I propose," "I claim." Of course, once you have claimed something you have to back it up with reasons or evidence. When you make assumptions or commitments for which there is no supportive reasoning, do so openly and clearly. Let the reader and yourself see what is to be argued for and what is to be accepted for the sake of the argument.

Are you habituated to casting your points in an interrogative mold? Do you know that such a presentation can be used to excess and thereby weaken your points? Do not use rhetorical questions, such as "Since when does the equality of all men not include women as well?" Rhetorical questions do not advance your philosophical argument but instead act as barbs against another party, sometimes the reader. If you put your questions in declarative form, such as "The equality of all men also extends to women," this requires you to support what you have asserted or to stand by it as an assumption.

Don't fight words; work with concepts and tackle arguments. Don't mince words; call a spade a spade. Every profession and academic field has its jargon, which is an unnecessary technical language applied to a subject in such a way that it cannot be understood by a layman. Use a technical term only if it helps in ways that ordinary language does not. In writing philosophy technical terms can provide shortcuts and identify special problems. But if used improperly they can conceal reasoning and confuse the issue. Use technical terms at your own risk (for a discussion of technical language in philosophy see ch. 5).

You can't depend on an aural grasp or an oral shaping of words in formal writing where a visual apprehension and a manual shaping are needed. Consider the following utterances:

The whole is greater than some of its parts.

The whole is greater than the sum of its parts.

In sum, these are wholly different ideas though in great part they sound the same. In writing do not confound these important words which sound alike and have Anglo-Saxon spellings: *through, thorough, throughout, though, threw, throw*. Though you knew what these meant when you threw them down on paper, it is worth being thorough, so before you are through go back through your writing to see that they are used correctly throughout, for otherwise you might throw away the meaning. The shortcut spellings "thru" and "tho," which have a certain current usage in traffic signs and newspapers, are not accepted in formal writing at present.

There are other errors of this kind due to the grasping of words as heard rather than as read or built with one's own hand. They are mostly trifling mistakes but they can throw into doubt the entire sense of your passage. In writing be careful to distinguish: *formally* and *formerly*; *form* and *from*; *causal* and *casual*; *quite, quiet,* and *quit*; *cite, site,* and *sight* (you can cite Aristotle, you can sight Athens; Athens is a site and Athens is a sight!); *proceed* and *precede* ("I have read the Proceedings of the preceding philosophy congress"); *precedent* and *president* (there is a precedent for the impeachment of a president); *later* is not *latter*, though *latterly* may be later than you think; *principal* (the main point) and *principle* (the starting point); *perform* and *preform*; *insight, incite,* and *in sight* (keep this difference in sight, that insight stirs within and incite stirs without); *idol, idyll, idle, ideal* (make up your own witticism for this set).

It's the case that *its* and *it's* are troublesome. *Its* is a possessive personal pronoun which does not require an apostrophe, e.g. "its meaning is clear." *It's* is a contraction for the subject and verb *it is*, which does require an apostrophe. The older form of the contraction for *it is* is *'tis*, which sports its apostrophe before the *t* rather than after it. Now explain the pair *theirs* and *there's*.

There's a growing neglect of the apostrophe to show possession in singular or plural nouns (excluding pronouns). The apostrophe is not heard in the spoken language and it is but a small mark on paper, yet it plays a very important function in identifying your written subject and its relationships. The difference between *gods' understanding* and *god's understanding* is the difference between polytheism and monotheism. The possessive apostrophe is in danger of becoming extinct in English. The loss will be yours (or do you think it should be *your's? yours'? you're? your? yore? yourn?*).

But is a strong word, one of the strongest in philosophy. It introduces a counterclaim. Do not use it more than once in a sentence; otherwise you weaken the force of the claim you are offering and obscure the point you are challenging. When you introduce a *but* claim, make sure the claim it is countering is clear. Similarly, for the sake of clarity in reasoning and in emphasis, use the following introducers of explanatory clauses no more than once each per sentence: *because, since, for, though.* Words with conclusive power—*therefore, thus, hence*—should also be used sparingly, perhaps no more than once to a paragraph. *Also* is not an argumentative connective; it is merely accumulative. Also it deflates emphasis.

When you find yourself writing *if, either,* or *both* in a sentence, make sure that you get to completing the connective with *then, or,* or *and,* respectively. Similarly, if you open with *on the one hand,* be sure to get to *on the other hand*. If you say, "There are two reasons, the first of which is . . . ," please signal when you get to the second reason. If there are several reasons or much space between them, then number them: (1), (2), (3), etc. In speech and informal writing we do not take such care with our connectives because the sense is usually implicit. But in philosophical writing it pays to make our steps in reasoning with explicitness, firmness, and clarity.

In dealing with the ideas of authors you have a choice of tense. Thus, "Aristotle said . . ." and "Aristotle says . . ." are both correct. In discussing ideas in terms of their philosophic worth, the present tense is preferable, for the ideas come alive out of a text that is designated with the name of a person, such as Aristotle. Your writing is more lively in the present tense than the past. Where the emphasis is on the history of ideas and chronological sequence, the past tense is preferable. Thus, "Aristotle said . . . , but Augustine corrected this." Don't shift tenses unnecessarily in your discussion. Such inconsistency in temporal viewpoint can make the reader tense.

If your writing suffers from massive run-ons, your thinking is hemorrhaging. No sentence: no sense. Seek first aid in a composition course. Before you hand in a written assignment in philosophy eliminate all unnecessary words. If doing so obliges you to hand in a blank sheet of paper at least you will be intellectually honest. Be meticulous in penmanship and typing, no matter how little time you have, for what you write must be legible. "In action" is not "inaction." "Something" need not be "some thing." "Acute remark" is not "a cute remark." To slur words is to obscure their sense. Don't let putting words on paper run off with your ideas. If a word is worth writing, it is worthy of careful writing.

Latin abbreviations.   There are some conventions in writing that you should know for the sake of your reading and your writing. There are many Latin abbreviations or words which are timesavers when used in formal writing. You have probably seen them before without noticing them: *i. e., e. g., viz., v., sic, ibid., cf., et al.,* and *etc.*

i. e. (*id est*), "that is," introduces a clarification or specification.

e. g. (*exempli gratia*), "for example," introduces an example.

viz. (*videlicet*), "namely," introduces an identification.

v. (*vide*), "see," introduces a source.

sic, "such," is placed within brackets following a word in a quotation if the word is incorrect or unexpected. It indicates *you* have not made an error in transcription.

ibid. (*ibidem*), "in the same place," refers to a previously cited work. [There are a number of other abbreviations and words, such as *op. cit.*, *idem.*, *supra*, which are especially useful in making references. You will have to consult a reference handbook, e. g. Kate L. Turabian, *A Manual for Writers of Term Papers, Theses, and Dissertations* (Chicago: University of Chicago Press, "A Phoenix Book," 4th ed., 1973), to learn how to use them. Footnote references must be carefully organized and properly punctuated instead of thrown together haphazardly. Cf. *ibid.*, ch. 4.]

cf. (*confer*), "compare," introduces an item for comparison.

et al. (*et alii*), "and others," cuts short a listing, usually of persons.

etc. (*et cetera*), "and so forth." Note, the symbol for *etc.*, the ampersand—&—is not in fashion in the formal writing of this century. Eschew the ampersand.

References.   In formal writing *full reference credit must be given everything you cite or utilize.* Your thinking must be distinguishable by the reader from the contributions of others. If it is not, then you cannot be credited with having written your own paper. One must give credit where credit is due and not receive credit for the work of others. When a scholar submits his own work he expects it to be respected and judged for its own merits. While it may be used by the reader it is not to be pirated. This applies to the works you have read in preparation for your paper. Respect yourself by giving proper credit to others so that your writing may be assessed for its own sake.

Any quotation, paraphrase, or other utilization of the words or work of another must be given full credit. Make precisely clear just what it is that you have borrowed from the author and where it is in your text. Blanket acknowledgments are inadequate, because under them it is not possible to tell where your ideas begin and those of the author end. Failure to give exact reference credit for all such use of another's work constitutes the crime against scholarship known as *plagiarism.* Plagiarism can also be illegal. It may constitute sufficient grounds for expulsion from school. Consult the manual for students and the student honor code if there is one at your campus. If you don't know whether your school has an honor code you may already be in trouble.

Full reference credit, not merely a name or a book title, is required so that the reader, including yourself, can verify the citations. This may help the reader appreciate the original source in a new way or cause him to dispute your interpretation of it. There are a variety of conventions for presenting references: they can be incorporated parenthetically into the text, they can be placed at the bottom of the page as footnotes, they can be listed together at the end of the paper or chapter as notes. The placing of references in the margins is now out of style. Reference notes may be composed in short forms and longer ones. My preference is the longest form, since it will have the maximum information that can be of aid to the interested reader. Preferences in the form of notes vary among instructors, editors, and publishing houses. Composition and research handbooks will help you in the selection of your convention.

As a rough guide you can keep in mind that a reference should indicate who, what, where, when, and which. For a book this means *author, title, city* and *publisher, date,* and *page.* For a periodical the "where" of city and publisher is replaced by the *periodical title,* and the additional information of *volume* and *number* is included. Other appropriate items that might be included in book references are: subtitle, series title, edition, editor, translator, chapter, and section. In citations of classical texts it is customary to refer to the special divisions, such as book, part, chapter, section, verse, or line. Individual authors, such as Plato and Aristotle, may have a standard pagination for reference to their words.

Even references to a dictionary must be fully accredited. "According to Webster," "Webster says . . . ," are unacceptable since "Webster" is a title appropriated by many dictionaries. Indicate the edition and date of the dictionary, because such reference books are frequently revised. An old dictionary may fit only an old usage. Note that there are differences in North American and British usage and spelling. For example, to table a matter in discussion means . . . But you can look it up.

Quotation. Avoid unnecessary quotation. Your essay is an occasion primarily for you to speak for yourself. Quotation is a scholarly aid, but the philosophic thinking must be done by you. Quotation can put before the reader's eyes a crucial passage that holds a wealth of insight or argument which you can then analyze and critically evaluate. You may also find a passage that crystallizes a problem in such a way that it gives you a step forward in the right direction. Quotation should be used to substantiate unusual claims you make about an author's contribution, whereas ordinarily complete references would suffice. There is an art of making telling quotations which are forceful revelations. Like all arts it requires practice and judgment. *A quotation should meet these standards: accuracy, pertinence, fruitfulness.*

Quotation is no substitute for reasoning. Any argument or extensive passage that you quote must be suitably explained and critically evaluated. Your responsibility as a thinker on an issue does not end with an appropriate quotation but rather begins with one, since you must make clear what is meant and whether it is right.

A misquotation may rule out of consideration the entire passage, for if you can't be trusted in getting the words right, then you are to be distrusted in getting the sense right. Verify the accuracy of every quotation by checking each word and punctuation mark more than once. As a rule, do not change the wording, spelling, or punctuation of the original, though it may follow archaic, British, or idiosyncratic conventions. But do not use those conventions in your writing, even when discussing the passage. Thus, Hume's *enquiries* into *judgement* and *behaviour* ought not, by their styling, to alter your behavior in writing the judgments of your inquiry into his work. When there is something missing in the text, an error of grammar or spelling, or a needed identification to be inserted, you may amend the text by use of brackets (but not parentheses): [ ]. You may also delete digressions, parenthetical remarks, or long intervening sections that do not affect the meaning; all deletions are to be signaled by three ellipsis dots: . . . , preceded or followed by appropriate punctuation.

Mechanics.   Whether you type or handwrite your essay it must be completely legible. A word that is mistyped, garbled, unreadable, or missing may result in the reader's abandonment of the sentence. When writing leave a space between lines and double-space when typing. This gives you room to make insertions and gives the instructor room to make comments. Leave wide margins on both sides of each page (an inch and a half is reasonable) for further comments by the reader. These are also margins of error in which you can add corrections to your paper before submitting it. Leave ample space at the top and bottom of each page. All this empty space will make your text easier to read. It will be easier for you (and the instructor) to find things needing correction. Write on only one side of the paper and number all pages clearly at the top in consecutive order.

I recommend the use of a separate title page. It should contain the title of the essay, the title and number of your course (not just "Philosophy"), your full name (and student number if required), the date of the submission of the essay (including the year), and the names of the instructor and the institution. You should repeat the title of the essay at the top of the first page of your text but kindly do not repeat your name. This is for the convenience of those instructors who prefer to read the assignments without knowing who wrote them, by turning back the title pages.

Notes to the text, whether they are for explanatory or reference purposes, may be written on a separate sheet and placed at the end of the essay or else written at the foot of the appropriate pages. If you adopt the latter procedure be sure you leave yourself enough room on each page for fitting in the notes without cramping them. If extensive reading has been done for the paper, a bibliography is in order. An index is not needed unless you write a book. A table of contents might be appropriate for a very long term paper which has distinct chapters.

Fasten all the pages together in consecutive order. You may staple them in the upper left corner. But if the notes are on separate pages and must be brought alongside the text by the reader, it is unwise to permanently fasten them to the text. A paper clip is the standard non-permanent essay fastener. Please do not join the pages together by merely folding and tearing a corner. You may also use prefabricated covers to hold the pages, but be sure the separate note pages can be easily removed. Such folders are attractive but I find them difficult to keep open while writing comments on papers. They also swallow margins.

After writing. When you have finished writing your paper *do not hand it in*. Do something more intellectually daring: read it. As you read you can correct those minor faults that usually find their way into lengthy writing. Correct typing or handwriting, catch misspellings, verify quotations once more, smooth out the style, double-check punctuation, adjust the tense. But you should also be reading in order to find faults in the reasoning:

Are there any points that are unclear?
Have you left out steps in the argument?
Is sufficient support given to your contentions?
Did you give a fair hearing to the views you oppose?
Have you exposed the problem so that the reader can see just what is at issue?
Have you resolved anything?
Do you see objections to be raised against your resolution?

You are the critical reader of your paper before the instructor becomes one. You have the chance to revise it and correct its faults. This will save the instructor some work and it allows you to hand in something closer to what you want to say.

As you read ask yourself, "Is this what I really had in mind? Does this say what I really have to say?" Sometimes you will find a gap between what you have in fact written and what you thought or think.

This can lead you to revise the paper to make it more representative of your thought, but it can also result in the revision of your thought to make it compatible with what you have succeeded in arguing on paper. It is possible, then, to teach yourself by writing. Unfortunately, we are often so enchanted by what we have written that we do not have the heart to approach it critically. "I have gone through all this trouble of writing it," we tell ourselves, "so there is no need to change it."

Therefore, re-read your paper a number of times. Allow some time to elapse between readings so that you will bring a fresh mind to its consideration. Approach the paper with patient objectivity, with desire for improvement, with willingness to criticize. Be prepared to object to your own work. Writing philosophy can become the dialogue of thinking rather than simply the expression of thought. You will need time for this rethinking and re-reading, with its possibilities for rewriting. Plan on a few days between the completion of the writing and the submission date of the paper. Do not hand in anything you have written which has not been subjected to your own critical scrutiny.

Receiving the essay back.   Your writing assignment does not end the moment you hand your paper in. You have still much to learn from it. It will be read critically by your instructor, corrected and commented upon, given a grade, and then returned to you. You may be tempted to read only the grade and dispose of the paper. Don't do it.

Once you have gotten over any exhilaration or disappointment occasioned by the grade, sit down in private and calmly study your paper. *Study* of it involves a number of readings. First, read the essay through as it was submitted to refresh your mind about what it constitutes. Quite a time may have transpired since you last read it. Hence, you may find that the essay as read by the instructor was not quite what you thought you had written.

Second, read it in the light of the instructor's comments. He may have written a few general sentences on the title page or last page, summing up his view of the entire paper; or a running commentary within your text; or question marks and crosses next to certain statements without specifying why these are dubious or incorrect. Criticism is not intended as discouragement but as encouragement to use your intellect. And don't let praise go to your head; just keep on using your head. Regard the paper as if it were written by someone else and join the instructor in its criticism.

Third, read the paper in an attempt to improve its thought as if it were only a draft for another paper which you could hand in:

How would you answer the objections or questions raised by the instructor (and yourself on re-reading)?

If you started another essay on this problem from scratch, what should you do the second time that would produce a better result?

If in a class discussion or on an exam you were asked about the very subject you wrote on, how would you effectively present the core of your contribution?

What did you learn about the problem by writing the paper?

What did you learn about writing philosophy by dealing with the problem?

Sometimes the instructor will discuss the returned papers in general in the classroom. You may then have the opportunity to raise questions and explore the problems of writing. If, after careful re-readings at home, you still do not see the significance of a comment or if you are still in doubt about how to proceed in philosophical writing, then arrange a conference with your instructor and bring the paper along.

Keep the term papers, exams, and all other written work that is returned to you. You can still learn from these assignments months afterward, even after the specific course. You may improve your writing over the whole course of your college years by frequent re-examination of what you have written. Even after college you may be fascinated to see some of the things you once thought. Everything you write is a chapter in the progress of your thinking.

Passages for study

1. I still think that I should continue to write everything that I consider important as soon as I discover its truth, and do so with as much care as if I intended to publish it. In this way I will have additional opportunities to examine my ideas, for doubtless we always scrutinize more closely that which we expect to be read by others than that which we do for ourselves alone, and frequently the ideas which seemed true to me when I first conceived them have appeared false when I wished to put them on paper. [René Descartes, *Discourse on Method*, trans. Laurence J. Lafleur (Indianapolis, Ind.: Bobbs-Merrill, "Library of Liberal Arts," 1956), Pt. VI, p. 42.]

2. It is usually not until I put on paper or into practice the theories I hold, that I truly understand them. [Student comment.]

3. Papers tend to force one to organize his usually scattered thoughts, discipline himself to work steadily, and evaluate his stance on a work. [Student comment.]

4. By disagreeing with others and committing my dissent to writ-

ing, I am, in fact, laying myself open to be criticized by many. He who speaks is judged merely by one or a few persons; whereas he who writes thereby exposes himself to criticism by all, and appears before the tribunal of the whole world and every age. [John of Salisbury, *The Metalogicon*, trans. Daniel D. McGarry (Berkeley. Cal.: University of California Press, 1962), Bk. II, ch. 18, p. 117.]

5. I had the impulse to write, to try a little different approach but held back because if it didn't follow the right track, my grade would be hurt, possibly failure. School is too expensive for failure. I did not allow myself to experience true learning. [Student comment.]

6. The more perfectly one's style fits the inner man and reveals its strength and defect, the clearer it becomes that the problem of style is not a problem of words and sentences merely, but of being the right kind of mind. [Brand Blanshard, *On Philosophical Style* (Bloomington, Ind.: Indiana University Press, "A Midland Book," 1967), p. 69.]

Bibliography

Bernstein, Theodore M. *The Careful Writer: A Modern Guide to English Usage* (New York: Atheneum, 1965).

Berry, Dorothea M., and Martin, Gordon P. *A Guide to Writing Research Papers* (New York: McGraw-Hill, 1971).

Matczak, Sebastian A. *Research and Composition in Philosophy* (Louvain: Nauwelaerts, "Philosophical Questions Series," 2nd ed., 1971).

Perrin, Porter G. *Writer's Guide and Index to English*, rev. Karl W. Dykema and Wilma R. Ebbitt (Chicago: Scott, Foresman, 4th ed., 1965).

Strunk, William,. Jr., *The Elements of Style*, rev. E. B. White (New York: Macmillan, "Macmillan Paperbacks," 1962).

Note: For reading materials to be used in conjunction with a writing assignment in philosophy, see the bibliography in ch. 8.

7

Examinations in Philosophy

Purpose. Examinations are usually thought of as devices for assigning grades to students for purposes of credit in a course. Exams generally do serve in this way, especially final exams. But they also have other functions. A good exam, like an essay or term paper assignment, is part of the *learning experience* in the course. In philosophy, exams are a healthy mental exercise.

Exams differ from other writing assignments in the restriction of time, sometimes to no more than an hour on a specific day, and in the source of the problem to be written on: you are told what to discuss. Thus, you probably do not know what the question will be that you have to write on. Moreover, you may not like the question—that is, if you had a choice you would not spend your time working on that problem. In an exam taken in class you cannot begin reading works by philosophers on the subject or hold discussions with other people in order to clarify your thoughts as you might do with a term paper. You have to do your thinking right there in the exam situation. And what you write down has to be handed in without the opportunity to muse over it through several re-readings. Hence, an exam is an intense writing experience requiring extra alertness and sharp intellectual activity.

In this way an exam is similar to class discussion. In both you have to be ready to formulate an intelligent position on an issue that comes up unexpectedly. But in discussion you have the assistance of fellow-discussants, while in an exam you are entirely on your own. Also, in writing for an hour or so, you are expected to give closer support to what you advance than in a brief discussion. But we know that writing takes longer than speaking. Hence, you will have to be more rigorous than in discussion though in a more limited time. In discussion you can always speak again to clarify or justify your position, but in writing you must provide such clarification and justification in the first place wherever it is needed. To do the work of the exam properly you will have to be selective and use your time and effort carefully. *Appropriate preparation for an exam is presumed on the part of the student.*

Preparation.   How does one prepare for an exam? The best way is through *development throughout the course of those philosophical skills* which are discussed in preceding chapters. You can't meet the exam on the proper footing if you have not been doing the coursework. Reading through the required texts the night before an exam might give you a familiarity with the material of the course, but if you haven't been working on that material in the course you will not have the skills available to do well on the exam.

You can prepare for an examination by *examining yourself*. Ask yourself what questions might appropriately be on the exam. Then proceed to tell yourself how you would deal with them. Some projected questions may be ones you are not ready to deal with. Give these your time and get yourself ready for them. Just as you must look ahead to the potential issues and directions of class discussion, so you can foresee what the exam could hold in store. This way you may actually recognize on the exam a question which you have already thought out. You can then proceed with confidence to rapidly write out your analysis and resolution. Sometimes the instructor will even ask the students to submit questions for an exam. Notice that by examining yourself beforehand not only do you practice problem-solving for exams but you also gain a firmer grasp on the problems of the entire course. Your self-examination in preparation for a formal examination is a re-examination of the course.

Before taking a new exam be sure to go over all your *previous exams and written work* in the course with an eye to remedying weaknesses. Don't be exclusively concerned with errors of content and accuracy (what you say), but be attentive as well to how you say things: the presentation of your analysis, the arguing of your position, the expression of your judgment. Think of how your writing may better serve your thinking.

Reviewing the readings is a traditional way of preparing for exams. But the exam in philosophy is not of the readings; it is of you. It is what you do with the readings that counts. Don't simply stuff your head with them; exercise your mind upon them. The best review of readings consists in thinking about them. You may need to re-read a few that have slipped your mind or that have been especially difficult. But if you try to re-read everything in the course prior to the exam you may be burdening your mind and making difficulties for yourself.

Though you should be aware of the contributions of the readings, it is more important that you be *aware of the problems*, for it is about these that reading and reflection, lecture and discussion, have revolved. Preparation for a philosophy exam means resolving the problems of philosophy as fully as you can. As you prepare for the exam you find it a microcosm or mirror of your work in philosophy.

Variety of exams. *There are different kinds of philosophy examinations.* It is not simply that the questions and the formats can differ. Since the exam addresses a certain stage of intellectual development, its function and nature will vary with the skills tested. Thus, a philosophy exam given six weeks into the term is not the same exam given in the second week even if the questions are identical. Exams are not interchangeable requirements spaced out along the way of the course. They are varied educational experiences within the context of the course. Every exam is unique. This is probably so even if it is given from year to year or to several classes a term, for each class is different in some way and the exam may have different meaning for the progress of each. It is likely that you will have more than one philosophy exam during the term, and that is desirable.

You may not know how to prepare for the first philosophy exam you take, how to work on it, and how to make use of it afterward. This chapter should clear up some of these troubles, but there is only so much you can be told in advance about taking a philosophy exam. Moreover, all of it is not equivalent to what you can learn by taking an exam. After you have had one you will better understand what is required, though the next one is likely to differ in its difficulties for you. You will have to prepare for each exam with the skills and insights available for it at that time in the course. A good exam draws you on to the exercise of skills or the tackling of problems that you had not been previously prepared for. An exam is not only a test of what you have already accomplished but also an accomplishing of what you had not been quite ready to do. Thus, no matter how well you are prepared for the exam in philosophy, an experience of innovation and discovery awaits you.

The most mature philosophical exam, especially the final, requires critical thinking and the original resolution of disputed issues. Such exams are not factual. Purely factual points about the material (e. g., "What is Gandhi's definition of *satyagraha?*") may be called for in brief quizzes in order to keep you on your toes and to make sure you are reading carefully. During the beginning and middle of the course you may be asked on an exam to expound or explain the arguments of some author. This is to see if you are developing analytic skills in reading and argument. But a philosophy exam may also question you on what has not been "covered" in class or "assigned" as homework. That is, instead of asking you about material or reading it may ask you about the thinking you should have been doing.

On some exams you are likely to be asked to resolve a problem. Here you must be ready to make a stand, to evaluate major contributions, and to designate what is best in a controversy and support it. The instructor will not be rating the particular stand you take against his own glimpse of the truth; rather, he will be critically evaluating the success of your reasoning in support of whatever you stand up for. It is taken for granted that you may not be sure of your position; offer the best you can. After an introductory philosophy course you may not be sure of anything. The commitments you make evident in your exams, like those in your class discussion and other written work, are expected to be the most reasonable that you can present at the time. An exam is not an inquisition.

Exams should be no great mystery. Worry centered on what the questions might be is unnecessary. You should be able to imagine what the questions will be; that is part of your preparation. And it is the way you answer them that counts. The old joke about philosophy is that the questions remain the same year after year while the answers change. Take that to mind. In some courses I have distributed the questions for the final exam at the first class meeting. The students then prepare for the exam by taking the course, but that is not different from the usual requirement.

Exam formats. There are closed-book, open-book, take-home, and make-up exams, and quizzes. Try to ascertain in advance under which conditions the exam will be given, for they involve differences of conduct during the exam and usually differences of preparation.

Closed-book exam. The *closed-book exam* means that you may not utilize textbooks or other books, notes and papers, reference works, recordings, or diagrams during the exam. Kindly do not bring any such materials to the exam room. If you have them in the room, do not have them at your seat. If you have them at your seat, do not have them opened. If you have them opened, you are not taking a closed-book exam.

The closed-book procedure obliges you to put aside the supports and distractions of other minds and other wordings so that you can concentrate on putting your own mind to the writing. The one essential thing you must bring to the closed-book exam is an open mind. See that your mind is prepared and responsive, and you won't miss the baggage left behind. It is understood that on a closed-book exam you cannot be exact in your references, it is unlikely you will quote anything, and you will not have as brilliantly formulated a wording as if you were permitted to use your notes.

Open-book exam. The *open-book exam* allows you to use your text-book and usually other books, as well as your own notes. If you can make good philosophical use of various books and of your notes in the short time allowed, so much the better. But what is still under examination is the resources of your mind. You should make your mind an open book; that's where the answers must come from.

The advantages of the open-book exam should be clear: you can double-check and make precise a reference and even quote with accuracy a telling passage; you can refresh your mind by referring to your notes and even utilize some of the wording you have worked out before the exam. If you are allowed to introduce reference works, a dictionary may help not only with the question but with your writing. Ascertain just how open the open-book policy is: whether it is unlimited in permissible materials or restricted, say to your textbook. My class once asked me to schedule a proposed unrestricted open-book exam in the campus library. They explained quite logically: "That would be much easier for all concerned than moving the contents of the library into the classroom."

There are hazards in taking an open-book exam that you should bear in mind, especially in philosophy. You may become befuddled by having too many books with you to consult instead of consulting the problem itself and your understanding. A philosophy exam is a thinking occasion, not a challenge to look things up. There is no time to learn about a problem by reading while you are supposed to be dealing with it in writing. The more you have to turn to the open books the less prepared you are.

Even if you do find helpful material in time, you may be so taken with it that you forget your primary task in the exam: using your mind. If you have your class notes at hand, the temptation will be to transfer them directly to the exam booklet (see the rehash method, below). If you have available all sorts of information about an author or a problem, the temptation will be to put it all down whether relevant to the question or not (see the kitchen-sink method). If you come across an excellent treatment of another problem, the temptation will be to write it up instead of the one asked about; and if you can find nothing helpful in the books, the temptation will be to stall, fight the question, and otherwise escape answering (see the cut and run method). Unless you learn to resist these temptations, you will probably defeat yourself on an open-book exam.

Philosophy differs from other disciplines in which you are examined in that it relies only in a minor way upon a body of special facts which can be looked up. In history the dates, in science the formulae, in technology the procedure, in social science the compiled data, in language the vocabulary can be fruitfully sought out in books or notes and put to use as relevant information. But philosophy specializes in not having specialized information. The philosophical examination is of your thinking more than of your information.

Think twice, then, before you burden yourself with materials at an open-book exam in philosophy. If you do quote, paraphrase, or otherwise utilize material not your own you are responsible for full identification of the sources. It is essential that your work be clearly distinguished from anyone else's work. An open-book policy is not a license for plagiarism. (Consult the section on references in ch. 6.)

Take-home exam. A *take-home exam* is one you do on your own time in your own surroundings, and presumably with the use of your books and notes. You have more time for the take-home than the hour or two of an in-class exam. Students often complain that time runs out in class just at the point where they are about to triumph in answering the question. On the take-home exam it is expected that you will stick to the problem until you have triumphed. You will also have time to pause during the exam at home, to re-read your work, even to rewrite it in a fresh draft. Hence, your work done at home is expected to be well written and maturely presented.

Take-home exams are generally assumed to be open-book, so that you may have time for thorough reading on a topic before you start to answer the question. Thus, the take-home relieves you of some of the tensions—the time pressures, the memory lapses, and the fishing for words—of exams in class. It gives you several advantages, but you are expected to make good use of those advantages. The take-home must be a more thoroughgoing, profound, polished, and carefully reasoned work than what you could do in class. Consequently, it may be a more difficult and time-consuming activity than taking an exam in class.

You have limited time for the take-home exam. It may be due overnight or in a couple of days, rarely more than a week. Yet you have lots of other things to do: other intellectual obligations and your personal commitments. You may not have a few hours to spare unless you carefully set them aside for the exam. And you may not feel like doing the exam when you have the time free unless you force yourself. I have long suspected that many take-home exams are written between midnight and five in the morning of the day they are due. You may not have a room to work on it without distraction and interruption; you may have to do it in the library. A take-home exam can bring home to you the sloppiness in your study habits. It may cause you to examine your efforts, your use of time, your self-motivation.

The ground rules for the take-home exam are generally assumed but some points are worth making explicit: When you receive the exam to take home you are considered to have begun it and are obligated to return it when due. Failure to return it by the appointed time may mean failure of the exam, just as if you did not hand in an in-class exam at the end of the class period. While the take-home exam almost always allows you to consult books, it does not allow you to consult other persons, unless authorized by the instructor. Thus, collaboration on the exam with others in the course or outside the course is ruled out.

Make-up exam. A *make-up exam* is a special exam administered to individuals who have missed a regular exam or important parts of the coursework or who are required to be re-examined because of unsatisfactory work. Make-up exams are extraordinary. They are a hardship for the instructor and a privilege for the student. They are not a right unless officially stipulated to be so by the institution's rules on certain kinds of absences. Do not count on taking one, though you may be required at some time to take one. If you have missed an exam or extensive parts of the course, it is at the instructor's discretion to decide whether a make-up exam is appropriate. The hardship consists in designing specifically for you an exam comparable to the one designed for the whole class. Since you will have had more time for study in the course than your classmates who took the exam before you, your version is not at the exact level and cannot be judged quite the same. A student taking a make-up has had the opportunity to learn from his classmates what the regular exam was; there may even be an in-class discussion of the corrected exam. For all these reasons, make-up exams have traditionally been more difficult than the assignments they make up for. Hence, they require more study and more intense writing than ordinary exams.

Students who are very weak in certain skills important to the course may be invited or required to take a make-up exam to give them an opportunity of doing better. This means extra work for both instructor and student. Such a make-up is likely to be the exception rather than the rule.

Quizzes. A philosophical *quiz* is an exercise to keep you on your toes. It is a stimulus to keep up with the work, and it makes you respond with alertness to points you should have encountered. A quiz is short: fifteen minutes may suffice; yet it can cover a lot of ground. The answers are short and may consist of one word or the circling of a correct item among multiple choices. There can be room for you to write out an answer but you will have to do so concisely. Quizzes only skim over philosophy, touching on details and relying on identification of positions. They do not get into the underlying complexities of profound problems, nor do they give you the opportunity to argue at any length with originality.

What you can learn from a quiz is whether you are paying enough attention to your work, whether you are doing it on time, and whether you are coming to class with a prepared mind. The quiz is useful to the instructor, for it tells at a glance the pulse of the course. It is quickly administered and quickly corrected. It will show the instructor whether the class is keeping up with the assignments, developing skill in recognizing issues, and having a care for accuracy.

A quiz now and then is a good exercise. Often quizzes are announced a day in advance, but part of the value of a quiz is its sudden occurrence. Instructors reserve the right to give a quiz at any time without prior notice. My students once angrily protested when I proposed a quiz toward the end of a class hour. "What's the matter?" I asked. "Why, we've just had a quiz at the beginning of the hour!" "Well," I rejoined, handing out the questions, "you should have learned something since then."

Practical hints. Get to the exam room a few minutes earlier than the scheduled exam so that you can get settled: make yourself comfortable, arrange your writing materials, and breathe more easily. Rushing to an exam interferes with your intellectual composure. Never expect to be given additional time because of starting late. Bring to the exam sufficient and dependable writing instruments. Pens with ink are standard; sharpened pencils may be permitted. If you are to bring the exam booklet or writing paper do so in adequate supply. Left-handed writers should make advance arrangements with the instructor for suitable desks or writing surfaces. It is wise to have your own timepiece with you, as there may not be one in the exam room. Sometimes the examiner will announce the passage of time; don't count on it. Please do not ask how much time remains in the exam: the distraction causes everyone else to lose time.

Cheating.   There is only one word I can give you concerning cheating on exams: *Don't.*

Thinking exams through: the problem.   *Begin with the problem.* Study the question carefully. See exactly what it calls for; also note what is not specifically called for. The exam question may pose a sharply delimited issue for you to work on. In working on it be sure to stay within the confines of the issue until it is resolved. Then you may show its larger significance and ramifications if there is time. The exam question may be quite general. *Warning:* a general answer might be so superficial as to get nowhere in particular and prove nothing of significance. You do not have the time to go through all the major points concerning a general problem. Therefore, limit yourself to the most important point or two and do a thorough job. If you find any time left you can take up another point or generalize concerning the problem as a whole. Being given a general topic means being challenged to choose a problem that you can treat with thoroughness within its scope.

You may come to the exam expecting to be given all the questions, for which you will merely supply answers. In philosophy you will also have to formulate the questions for yourself to a certain extent. Some exams offer a choice of questions to be answered. Thus, before you do any answering, do some questioning. Narrow down what is proposed to the exact problem you can meaningfully treat in the short time available. Take note of any materials that the exam questions ask you to consider when answering. As you study a question you are perforce studying the problem itself as one you are to deal with. As the latter becomes clear you can decide on the direction which your discussion should take.

I have heard a frequent student complaint about exams and philosophy courses in general: "I do not know what the instructor wants from me." I shall now tell you: The instructor wants what is true or your very best efforts to arrive at it, by the fullest use, made evident, of your skills of analysis, inquiry, argument, and judgment. What more can an instructor ask of you? Can you want anything less than this of yourself?

As you are analyzing the selected issues and planning your treatment of them, it may be helpful to make a note of the points to be covered. There probably is not enough time to draft an outline if you are writing in class. But you should have an idea of the essential matters you ought to deal with, even if you are not quite sure how you will deal with them when you get to them. The force of the inquiry or argument should shape such points when you arrive at them in your writing. All this planning should take place before you write. Think before you write is an excellent maxim in philosophy. So is: Think while you write. As well as: Think after you write. For an hour question on an exam you may fruitfully spend ten minutes in thinking out what to write before you begin to do so. In that way you will have given yourself the scope and direction needed for the writing. That does not mean that the writing merely expresses those few minutes of thought. Rather, the writing becomes a continuation of the initial thinking. *Writing actualizes thought.*

Putting words on paper.   Write fluently. Use simple and direct language. Develop your points one by one with clarity. Avoid long sentences which can entangle your points and make you pause to straighten them out. Keep advancing in your reasoning; don't get bogged down in digressions, weighty examples, terminological prolegomena (or big words). As you write what you think, you will think what you write. The interplay between thought and word is a creative advance in the intellectual activity that constitutes writing. The "answer" is not just something you possess in mind and transfer to paper; the "answering" is the crucial engagement of mind on paper, the process of thinking making itself evident. Hence, expect discovery and difficulty as you write. Don't avoid the latter; head for it. Philosophy navigates toward the rocks. If difficulties are discovered in the course of reasoning, discoveries are made in the direct confrontation of difficulties. *The philosophy exam is an adventure in thinking under the imperatives of time.* Be courageous in the pursuit. Cleave to clarity no matter how beclouded the sailing. Pause now and then to re-read what you have thought: this can suggest new directions to pursue as well as corrections to previous pursuits.

Slap-dash method.   There are a number of things to avoid in exam writing. The *slap-dash method*, known alternately as the hodge-podge or mish-mash method, consists in putting words down so rapidly and so carelessly that they do not make sense when read. If you abbreviate everything you can and some things you cannot, throw in dashes instead of punctuating, link up everything with ampersands, string together phrases without making sentences, and present your essay-length answer as one undifferentiated paragraph, then it is below the level of acceptability. Because an exam has a time limit does not mean you may abandon all the standards of correct English. Your writing must be legible and intelligible before the reader can understand and assess what you think. This "sentence" comes from an exam on the critique of metaphysics by Logical Positivism and will illustrate slap-dash. The passage may have been quite intelligible to its author at the moment of writing it:

> The imperical method of siense superior to that of metaphysics for its' correct meaning—veryfiability—is more meaningful and their was not the usage of the word existance, absolute or nothing according to the "Vienna Bunch as there is in the other which is there for wrong.

Kitchen-sink method. Avoid the *kitchen-sink method* of writing exams. This consists of dumping everything you know or have heard about into your answer no matter what the question calls for. For instance, the question may be to critically evaluate Descartes' claim about his own existence. You might write on Descartes' claim about God's existence, Descartes' contribution to mathematics, and Descartes' school-days, and you might be quite accurate in everything you say and quite judicious in all your evaluations, yet you may fail the exam, for your answers have not been to the point of the question. A philosophy exam is not a dragnet spread to catch the quantity of your information. It is the quality of your reasoning that counts. Part of the challenge is to address your reasoning to a particular issue.

Rehash method. The *rehash method* consists in tossing back at the instructor everything he has ever said on the subject insofar as you were able to transcribe it and commit it to memory. The assumption is that since it came out of the instructor's mouth it must be good, because he is being paid to say it, and he must recognize its worth when recast. In this way you get the instructor to answer his own question. But what he asks is for you to answer. Your answer must be the fruit of your thinking. You may not have done any thinking on the problem if you were preoccupied with transcribing and later memorizing the words of the instructor. Philosophy instructors are not flattered or pleased to read their own views rehashed and served back to them. They are disappointed that the student has not taken the views into serious enough consideration to think them out and thereby arrive at the student's own views. "I am not training parrots," a colleague once told his class, "but stimulating intellects." Several students quoted this on their next exam.

Cut and run method.   The *cut and run method* consists in avoiding answering the question at all costs. Alas, too often students succeed in not answering the question. Sometimes this is done by attacking the question, the instructor, or the course. You may not like the question, you may well wish it had been posed differently or at a later date, but you still must do the best you can with it. Sometimes cut and run simply ignores the question asked and proceeds to answer some other question that the student is better prepared to deal with. Brilliant philosophic papers have been written in this fashion, though they result in failure of the exam. The term paper is a fit occasion for showing what you can do with a problem of your choice.

Cut and run also takes the form of running out of time, especially if the undesirable question is the last one on the exam or if it is a long one whose rewriting takes time. Instead of repeating the question start answering it. Exam questions are usually numbered so that you can identify your answers. Once I gave an exam with a question that was four pages long so that the students would have the maximum delimitation of the problem which they could then closely address without resorting to kitchen-sink or cut and run. Most of the exams submitted were largely condensed transcriptions of the question followed by its paraphrase.

Taking more time.   When the exam is over it is over. *Do not finish the sentence you are writing.* Close your exam booklet or prepare your pages to hand in. Please do not create problems by calling for "one more minute!" "three more seconds!" "two more words!" This is unfair to the instructor, who has devised the exam for a certain time limit, it is unfair to your classmates who have completed their work in the proper time, and it is unfair to those who cannot stay around another few minutes even if more time were granted. You may find yourself so intensely involved in writing as the exam concludes that you are most reluctant to stop and hand it in. Good, stop and hand it in. You may continue your writing on your own at home for the sake of finding the truth. You should learn to adjust your timing on exams so that you get into what you have to say earlier in the hour and thereby reach the heart of the matter before time is up.

Don't make the teacher play an authoritarian role by commanding you to hand in your paper after the exam has officially concluded. I know a shy teacher who is so adamant against playing such a role that he runs out of the building with the exams that have been turned in and jumps on his bicycle, requiring those who are "just finishing the last sentence" to chase after him across the campus. Less amusing is the case of another colleague not given to wrestling with students for their exams: whenever the exam was finally handed to her by someone who took extra time, she simply tore out the last page or so and handed it back to the student.

Personal pleas.   Students should not write excuses, apologies, pleas, or other *personal notes* to the instructor in any exam or written assignment. Your formal writing should be allowed to speak for you itself without your speaking for it. Don't give personal pleas; don't get personal, please. An instructor coming across a passage like this:

> I know I did poorly on this paper and it is my own fault. But I just want to say how much I enjoyed taking this course. You're a great teacher. I hope you count my classwork more than this written assignment in the final grade.

might construe your comments as an effort to influence the assessment of your work in terms of personal interests rather than solely in terms of your work. Avoid even the appearance of influencing the instructor in such a manner. Instructors may lower the grade or fail outright any written work that makes personal appeals for leniency or special consideration. However, if you were unprepared for the assignment or exam due to reasonable circumstances, you might well explain this to the instructor in his office *after* the papers are graded and returned. Sometimes, by explaining before the day of the exam or due date of a paper the justifiable reasons for your unpreparedness, you may be given a delay in the assignment by the instructor. But that is hardly to be expected.

Generally, instructors regard it as the student's responsibility to prepare and complete all assignments when due. Instructors ought not to be asked to play Solomon by judging your excuses for not doing required work. Their task is to judge your work. If you are ill and cannot properly do an exam or assignment, then don't do it. Notify the instructor and submit a medical form. Some schools have regulations recognizing the right of students to make-up exams for attested medical reasons. *Once you decide to take an exam or submit a paper do so without excuses.* The instructor should read, criticize, and assess your philosophic writing by paying attention to the philosophy and not the person writing.

Receiving the corrected exam.   When the *corrected exam is returned to you,* the second half of your learning from the experience begins. You should do the same careful re-reading at home as required for essays that are returned (see *Receiving the essay back* in ch. 6). The grade teaches you nothing if you don't read the exam. Shouted whispers in the classroom as exams are returned of "What did you get?" and "How did you do?" cheapen the learning experience.

An examination *is* a competitive exercise. You strive with yourself to do better than you have done before and hence to go beyond your limits. The instructor measures your achievement against the level of skills he judges the class ought to have attained at that stage in the course. In his judgment the instructor may take into account the comparison between individual efforts and the general achievement of the class. The grade you receive is a qualitative sign that has reference to the instructor's judgment, your progress, and the class's level.

Many students find that they simply did not have enough time on the exam to clearly say all they meant to say. You have to learn by practice how much you can accomplish in a test situation. If you did poorly in an exam don't be discouraged. Use the returned exam as a lesson for improvement in your next exam. Don't be overly sensitive about the critical remarks on your exam. In college you've got to stand criticism and learn from it. If it seems the instructor loses his temper when putting down big *X*s or crossing lines out or writing "NO!" don't hold it against him. It is an excess of horror at error. The instructor may read dozens of papers at one sitting and thus grow a bit impatient. If you did very well on an exam don't be conceited, for you have missed the opportunity of having pointed out to you those skills you should now be improving. If there is more criticism than praise in the comments on most papers, it is because the instructor is especially concerned with pointing out what needs further work. If the instructor raises a question or objection to every point, that doesn't mean it is all wrong; this is a way of stimulating you to further thought.

If you are unduly uncomfortable in the exam situation, try to accustom yourself to it at home by writing practice exams. This is a good way to develop proper writing habits, it is effective as preparation for in-class exams, and it will serve as a model for work on take-home exams. You might as well get used to taking exams and to working under pressure: it is the occupational hazard of being a college student. Exams too often are considered threats, punishments, and inflictions of hardship by the authorities. Learn to understand them as part of your learning. *All philosophy is an examination in which we test our understanding by the challenges of problems.* What counts is not how well you do on the particular exam in your philosophy course but how well philosophy will help you in "the long examination which life sets us." [William James, *Talks to Teachers on Psychology* (New York: W. W. Norton, "The Norton Library," 1958), ch. 12, p. 101.]

Exams are usually discussed in class. After re-reading your returned paper at home you may wish to ask for clarification or help by the instructor. This often can be done in subsequent class sessions. If you can't get the help you need through your own efforts or with the aid of the instructor in class, then seek him in the office. Believe it or not the instructor may not recall your exam or essay by heart. Have it with you if you wish to discuss it with him.

Grades. The subject of greatest interest for some students in a course is grades. This is the subject of least interest to most instructors. This, then, is a ripe matter for misunderstanding and resentment. The instructor sees his task as contributing to the education of the students regardless of grades. Some students see their task as getting good grades regardless of their education. Concerning philosophy, one student confessed: "The subject is fine in itself, but due to the fact that grades are important to some of us, the course is not worth the frustration." Students hold it against instructors that they have a punitive power of giving grades which inhibits the educational efforts of the students. Instructors are tempted to use grades punitively in getting students to do their educational tasks.

What is essential to a course is not the grade but the work. Grades and credits are neither the goal nor the reward but evaluations of what you are doing. If your chief concern in a course is getting a high grade or a passing grade you will probably miss the point of the course, which is its educational value to you (consequently you may receive a poor grade). Asked what was wrong with a course in philosophy, one student replied: "The very fact that it is a course and as such is subject to educational obligations like exams and term papers and grade pressures." Get the most out of a course by meeting your educational obligations.

Students in philosophy ask: "How can you evaluate my work in philosophy?" "Who is to say what is right or wrong?" "Don't you simply reward those whose views you favor?" We can evaluate philosophy because that is what philosophy itself requires. The student is to say what is right or wrong but must argue the case for whatever he says. The instructor weighs not the mere outcome, what the student believes, but the reasoning the student presents. A high grade in philosophy is a sign not that you have found the right answers but that you have learned to discipline your reasoning in the search for truth, which includes the right questioning.

Sample exams

1. General Introduction. Mid-term. In-class.
Good morning. This is a 60-minute exam. Please write on any two of
the three following questions. You may not use your books or notes.
A. Berkeley says, "Things are Ideas." Explain how he arrives at such
a position. What difficulties does his account cause or resolve?
Critically evaluate his reasoning.
B. Does God exist? Give the best proof you know. Then raise appropriate critical doubts about this proof. Resolve the issue by either
overcoming the criticism or showing the inadequacy of the proof.
C. Prove that the chair you are sitting on is real. In what does its reality consist? How do you know?

2. General Introduction. Final. In-class. Closed-book.
Please answer both questions. You have an hour and a half.
A. Write your own question on a problem appropriate to the course,
and then answer it fully.
B. Resolve the philosophic dispute concerning either I or II:
    I. Freedom of the will.
    II. Proof of God's existence.

3. General Introduction. Mid-term. Take-home. Open-book.
In two days submit an essay on the mind/body problem. What is the
mind/body problem? What is the solution to it? In your answer analyze the principal features that constitute the problem and the leading
alternatives for resolving it. If you introduce the ideas of others be accurate and critical in your representations. In presenting your solution
to the problem show why it is preferable to the alternatives and how it
would withstand the objections raised by the alternatives. Use your
brain and put your mind to it.

4. Ethics. Mid-term. In-class. Closed-book. One hour.
Miss A: "Happiness is pleasure."
Mr. B. "No, happiness is virtue."
Please get into the discussion.

5. Philosophy of Science. Mid-term. In-class. Open-book. 75 minutes.

                                   space

Does it exist? Is it merely a concept? If it exists what is it? What is the proper concept of it? What is its role in physical science? If you introduce the theories of any of our authors do so critically.

6. *Oriental Philosophy. Final. Take-home. Open-book.*

Select from the following list one work which you believe has the greatest philosophic significance. Then elucidate and critically evaluate the philosophic contribution made by that work. Because of the limitations of time do not attempt to explain the whole work, but clarify and judge its essential contributions. Return your essay in three days.

    A. The Bhagavad-Gita.
    B. The Dhammapada.
    C. The Yoga Sutra.
    D. The Analects of Confucius.
    E. The Tao-te Ching of Lao Tzu.

7. *Existentialism. Final. In-class. Closed-book. 75 minutes.*

Rather than ask you a question to be answered, I am going to give you the answer today. This is my sincere position concerning the philosophic issues we have discussed. Your job is to examine the answer, to question it, to challenge it, and to support it where appropriate. The answer:

    You are human.

8

Philosophy in the Library

Intellectual activity. There are several good reasons for going to the campus library. It is above all a suitable place *to study and think.* While a library reading room may be a large public space filled with people busily engaged, yet it simultaneously may be a temple of interior privacy. No one knows what is going on in your head and no one is permitted to ask. This is essential for philosophic freedom. You may take your time here and follow the arguments where they lead without interruption or distraction. It is important that you have a secure place to think and read about philosophy. Usually, the hallways, the student lounge, the lawn, and your living-room at home will not do. In those localities people may ask what you are thinking, and that may inhibit your thinking. The library is the place for everyone in the college community, including your instructors, where reflection and reading may follow their private course. Here you may contemplate any absurdity with equanimity and press your thought with composure into the clouds of obscurity.

No one in the library should be able to see what you are writing; hence, you have another inestimable freedom in making notes, jotting down questions or strange ideas, and composing an argument on paper. You may read, write, and think at your own pace and in your own order.

If you have a room to yourself at home or in the dormitory you will have even more freedom than the privacy of the library affords: you can pace about, tear up pages of your notes, and throw your books against the wall when the going gets rough. But your room is also cluttered with personal belongings and all sorts of reminders of other business to attend to. It is tempting on occasion to turn on the radio, stretch out and take a nap, or start cleaning your shoes. Fortunately, you can't do anything like that in the library. You leave your baggage behind when you enter this asylum. The library encourages

144

work and reflection. There is time for daydreaming too. The library gives dignity to study and musing. If you aren't prepared for this you will find it a dreadfully boring place.

Facilities.   It is wise to *explore the library* and try out different locations within it for study. In addition to the large reading room there may be smaller study lounges. Individual study alcoves called *carrels* are sometimes available to undergraduates; here you can set up your work with notebooks, textbooks, and library books, and return to them daily. By moving about you will find a location that is not too noisy (or too quiet), has enough light and working space, and is comfortable in other ways. Don't give up on your college library as a place to study without having fully tried it. The American college library is one of our unsung national treasures. When I studied at the Sorbonne library I had to sit on the floor because the seats were quickly taken, and on winter afternoons I used my own flashlight in order to read.

In addition to study facilities the library also contains *books*. If you are reading a selection in a book of readings you might be interested in taking down the author's full text to see the continuation of his arguments. If you have some difficulties in following the text of a translation it is a good idea to look into a few other translations of the same work to see how they render the obscure passages. Further direct aid to your required reading is available in the library's reference works, such as dictionaries, encyclopedias, atlases, histories, which can clear up references and allusions in your text. The library houses secondary sources, explanatory and introductory works, and background information. The library has a world of material for you to use in writing your term paper. Finally, it has the resources for your further self-education in philosophy as you pursue problems whether touched on in the course or not. We will discuss in detail how to use the various library materials for these purposes.

Seeking aid.   When you are in trouble in a course the library is an excellent source of help. The library is the *college's intellectual first-aid station*. It is largely a self-service station. Though there are professional aids at hand, such as the card catalogue, the floor and shelf plan, and above all the librarians, it is you who must learn what the library can do to help you, where its materials are, and how to use them. You might as well find out early in your college years how to get such help, because if you don't have to go to the library for course help sometime, then you are missing something in your courses. Philosophy sends many students to the library.

A caution: *problems engender problems*. As you seek help you may become even more lost. Be aware of the risk, then, proceed carefully, and allow yourself the time to face new confusion. For instance, if you are having trouble understanding Berkeley's Immaterialism, you can go to the library to read explanatory material, but the first item you consult may not clear up all that puzzled you in Berkeley, the second may be of further help but in a different way, and by the time you have culled through six items you will have half a dozen differing and perhaps conflicting accounts. The more you read of secondary works in philosophy, as in literary criticism, the more divergent do the interpretations of the primary material become. The quantity of explanatory aids may only compound your confusion.

What counts is an explanation that you yourself test out and find to be reasonable in the light of your own reading and thinking. *You must be the judge of the worth of the helping hand in philosophy;* don't expect to be simply handed the right answers without thinking. So when you head for the library for help be prepared when you get there to help yourself. The test of whether you are helping yourself, say on Berkeley, is when the explanatory material leads you back to Berkeley's own reasoning to help you tackle it afresh to understand Immaterialism.

When you come to the library with a philosophic problem remember that the library contains more things than are dreamt of in philosophy, such as history, biography, literature, and religion. Make sure that what you read deals with the philosophic discipline rather than these other subjects (see ch. 1 on distinguishing philosophy from other disciplines). You can find out that George Berkeley was an Anglican bishop, that he believed in the marvelous properties of something known as tar water, that he penned the line

> Westward the course of empire takes its way; [George Berkeley, "Verses on the Prospect of Planting Arts and Learning in America," *Essay, Principles, Dialogues,* ed. Mary Whiton Calkins (New York: Scribner's, "Modern Student's Library," 1957), p. viii.]

and that he traveled to Rhode Island to set up a learned community. Not a whit of this will help you to understand Berkeley's theory of Immaterialism. Don't be distracted by interesting events, facts, personalities, influences. Seek understanding of the reasoning.

You and Berkeley must have a showdown. You can't rely on intermediaries to settle the issues at stake. They can give you some tips, point out some weaknesses, clarify Berkeley's approach, and suggest a response, but it is you who will have to confront Berkeley. Now if you don't know what Berkeley's Immaterialism is, head for the library and find out.

Term paper topic. You may not have any problem when you go to the library but you may try to find one there. *The library welcomes those in search of a term paper topic.* How do you find a topic? Well, what would you like to write on—what do you think is important for treatment and interesting to you? You might have some ideas, perhaps general or vague ones, or you might be undecided about going ahead with a specific topic.

If you go to the library with ideas in your head then you have a good start on getting the library to work for you. Take the ideas one at a time, perhaps one at a visit. Ask yourself what you would like the library to tell you about the idea. Do you want a broad survery of the topic to see its overall importance in philosophy? Are you interested in finding manageable subtopics of what is already a broad problem? Do you want an author or two who has written on the topic so that you can study his contribution? Or would it be better to get hold of three or four brief opposing views on the subject so that you can detect what is controversial in it? *The more closely you probe your aims the more shape do you give to your inquiry in the library.*

For the general survey, you might consult a chapter in an introductory volume or an encyclopedia article. To find authors addressing one another in controversy, you could consult anthologies or bibliographic indices. To find a single prominent author to work on, you may use the bibliographies in reference works, introductory volumes, or the card catalogue.

Be wary of getting into more material than you can handle. The library holds more material on certain topics than any person could read through in a lifetime. Keep in mind as you start your library visit how much time you have to write the paper, to think it out, to read for it, and to look around for what to read. This should suggest something about the number of items to consult, their length, and their level of difficulty.

Term papers in philosophy, unlike history, are not primarily research papers, so you do not have to go through the major works in the library's holdings. Since your term paper is not a report on material, what you are chiefly looking for in the library is a stimulus to your own philosophic thinking. The one library you cannot escape consulting when you engage in philosophic work is your own mind. The complaints "The library just had too much stuff on the topic for

me to get through in the time I had" and "I really couldn't find anything in the library to help me on my topic" both indicate a weakness
in the student's work rather than in the library's facilities.

Many times a trip to the library helps philosophy students to work
on a topic because they don't find anything there they can use. By discovering what doesn't fit in the treatment of the problem you narrow
down what you think does need treatment. By not finding an author
with a worthwhile position on a problem you can better identify what
you expect from a reasonable position and begin to develop that position. Instead of further clarification of the topic you had in mind, you
might have been dished up a fresh serving of confusion. Fight back by
restoring whatever clarity you saw to the problem and argue your
way from there, steering clear of the whirlpools of confusion you had
stumbled upon.

Your library visit may also have talked you out of your topic if
you found the topic gets you nowhere, that it is too difficult, that it
has been fully resolved by others, or else that it is far less interesting
and challenging than you thought. Be thankful that the library has
saved you all the time of working on the paper only to abandon it.
You may be disappointed by the quality of the treatments you find in
the library: not good enough to be built upon. Good for you; take that
as an encouragement for you to do better in the pursuit of truth. But
the treatments you find might seem too good, leaving no room for you
to make a new contribution. That's good too; when you find an argument that gets close to the truth, prove that it is sound, defend it
against objections, apply it, and see what its further implications are.

Suppose you have no idea in mind for the term paper when you
head for the library. You are heading for trouble. Better examine your
intentions. Are you hoping the library will somehow authoritatively
assign you a topic, getting you out of the predicament of choosing one
on your own responsibility? You won't find one posted or lying open
on a table. Nor will the librarian in lieu of your instructor give you
one. If you observe several philosophy books, articles, or entries dealing with some problem you may conclude it is an official problem and
one you can write on. But unless you have independently thought out
what the problem is, you will not be treating a problem. You've got to
tackle it from within the difficulty, not from the outer appearance that
it is problematic. Hence, you will be giving youself the topic though
you think the library gives it to you. Caution: There are on the library
shelves many, many problems philosophy has treated; therefore, you
will have to choose among them and not simply pick one up.

By going to the library, are you hoping just to see the spread of philosophic problems without expecting one to fall into your lap? This you can accomplish by browsing through books, glancing through reference works, looking at the table of contents of periodicals. Haphazardly you will see some of what is going on in philosophy. A title might catch your eye, an essay might interest you, an idea you had not considered before might be brought before your attention. But this is superficial. To see if there are any problems beneath the surface you will have to do some careful reading or some careful speculation. *A philosophic problem reveals itself only when your mind probes it.* This takes time, especially if you want to see a number of diverse problems. Don't be overwhelmed by the richness of topics; your present task is to deal thoroughly with one. (For further discussion of selecting term paper topics see ch. 6.)

Expanding understanding. The library is important not only when you need something required for the course such as a term paper topic or the clarification of class materials. It helps you with philosophy in the larger sense intended by the course: the *expansion of your understanding* by your own free exercise of it. The library allows you to follow up what interests you in the course, and it gives you the opportunity to work on issues not touched on in the course. The library is the simultaneous learning resource for all possible philosophy courses. Use it for your own sake. The library is the warehouse of philosophy's treasures. The key is your intellect.

Don't restrict your education to what is included in courses. Curiosity is the lifeblood of philosophy, and the library is a temple of curiosity. You may look into any book merely because it strikes your interest. Browse among the collections. A title alone may awaken your interest, such as *On Laughter* by Bergson, or *The Philosophy of "As If"* by Vaihinger. See what sorts of things are available for your private reading in philosophy. Just knowing that a certain book exists may be of significance.

Don't limit your browsing in the library to the philosophy section. Get an awareness of where books in different fields are located just as you are familiar with the location of the books on your own study shelf. You will find works that raise philosophical questions—for example, J. B. Bury's *The Idea of Progress* and Claude Bernard's *Introduction to the Study of Experimental Medicine.*

Of course, you have course requirements to meet and your time is limited. The library is always there ready for you. If you are not ready for it during the term, you might drop in later to continue your reading in philosophy. If during your college years you do not make use of the library for your expansion of understanding, then you will miss not only something important that the library offers but also something important that is a part of college.

Books.   *Philosophical books* are of two kinds: for the specialist or for the general reader. Some authors and publishers may not make that distinction clearly, but there are usually some signs by which you can judge the level of a book without reading it. Subtitles (e.g., "A General Introduction"), series titles (e.g., "Research Publications in Phenomenology"), and publication information (e.g., "originally presented as public lectures") can be revelatory. Such information is contained on the title page of the volume itself and on the entry card in the library catalogue; it may even be given in a bibliographic reference in some work you have consulted. The book jacket composed by the publisher's advertising staff will often tell you succinctly for whom the book is intended, though few libraries retain the jackets. However, the preface written by the author should make the purpose and level of the book quite clear. The preface is the author's calling card which lets you know whether or not a thorough acquaintance is worthwhile.

If it is a specialized book written chiefly for fellow-specialists then it is likely to prove far from useful to you. The excessive technicality (and hence lack of general comprehensibility) of current professional philosophy is not representative of philosophy's career, though there were similar obscurities in certain moments of Scholasticism. Up to the first decades of this century philosophers, especially those writing in English or French, wrote books and articles of intellectual sophistication that could be understood by people who had not graduated from college. Curiously, as philosophy prospered in the universities in Germany and then in America during this century, so did the gap widen between professional writing and general understanding. A result of this development is that you may find it easier to read the eighteenth-century author Berkeley, even with his strange reasoning, than to read an explanation of Berkeley's reasoning published in this decade. Whereas technical problems were once reserved for professional journals while books were written for readers in general, nowadays the chapters in many philosophical books were originally written as journal articles.

But suppose the book you hit upon is written so that you can understand it. Do you have time to read it? You may be hard put to find time to read the books required for your courses. Taking on an additional volume is a major undertaking. Think twice before reading a book. While reading it you may also have second thoughts and decide you are wasting your time. *There is no guarantee that reading any book will be of value to you.* At least you may learn that fact by having wasted your time. In your lifetime you can expect to read several books that aren't worth reading. Don't let that keep you from reading. There is a gamble in all intellectual exploration.

What is the best way to make use of your time in selecting and reading philosophic books? *Read with a purpose in mind.* For what reason are you looking for a book? What are you seeking in reading it? If you have a term paper topic in mind you may be looking for an original treatment of the problem to analyze as a beginning. Hints as to what books are available that treat such a topic may be found by looking carefully in your textbook, for its author or editor has probably mentioned pertinent books and offered a bibliography at the end of a chapter or section. By looking into some of these works you will find still other books cited by the authors or listed in their bibliographies. *One book leads to another.* Sooner or later every book is taken note of in another volume; in this way books keep one another alive. Try to get the sense of the inner life of the realm of books. This life is especially noticeable in philosophy, where it takes on the appearance of an enormous dialogue across the centuries, beyond boundaries, and in every tongue. By opening one philosophy volume you establish a listening post on the life of ideas.

Anthologies. One kind of book to keep your eye out for is the *anthology, which has already done the work of assembling materials* in a particular field or on a specific problem that you would otherwise have to locate separately. A good anthology will harbor a diversity of views on a subject so that the contrasts are stimulating and the important issues evident. An anthology can get you into the thick of the argument. Sometimes anthologies on problems are used as textbooks within a course.

But there may not be an anthology on the subject you wish to work on. If you do find one, it is unlikely you will have the time to read the whole work, so you must be selective in consulting it. You may find that the interesting selections are cut too short, which means you have to look up the original texts for further study. When you read a number of works in philosophy on a problem or area you may think of them as selections within the anthology of your mind.

Card catalogue. Another way to discover what books are at hand on a philosophic topic is to consult the *card catalogue* in your library under the topic. These cards are the identity papers of books. They tell the sharp-eyed investigator not only the author, title, and identification number, but the principal subjects treated, sometimes a table of contents, the date and publishing history, the origin of the contents, and the length. A few minutes' use of the catalogue can inform you about dozens of books without your having to examine them. You can jot down the call numbers of a few likely volumes and then seek them out. Just for the sake of curiosity go to the library today with a topic in mind and see what the catalogue tells you is in store.

But there are shortcomings in depending upon topical listings in the library. The topics selected by the librarians for inclusion are very broad ones, such as "Causality," while the narrower problems that you are interested in, such as the causality proof of God's existence, probably will not be found in the catalogue. A book which has only a few chapters on the specific topic you consult might not be listed under that topic.

A more time-consuming method of finding appropriate books which may lead to interesting discoveries is to go directly to the philosophy collection and look through the *table of contents* of volumes that catch your eye. This is haphazard procedure, yet it may be easier to decide what book to work on when you have a chance to pluck a few from the shelves and open them up on the spot.

The most systematic method of discovering the important books or articles on a topic is to consult the *bibliographies* of reference works, such as the *Encyclopedia of Philosophy*. Great care is usually taken in the preparation of such lists so that the reader will be guided to the essential works. However, this is no guarantee that you will understand all the works listed. The selective bibliographies of reference works and secondary sources are generally more useful than bibliographic indices, such as *Philosopher's Index* and *Reader's Guide to Periodicals*. The latter sources will list the largest quantity of items discoverable on a topic without indicating their importance.

Librarian.   One of the resources of any college library is the *trained librarian*. The librarian is not simply someone who checks out books for you and tells you not to make noise. In some institutions librarians have faculty status, for they are fellow-educators. They are experts on how to make use of learning materials: what resources exist, where they are located, how to obtain them. The librarian is stereotyped as a custodian of books; think of him as a valuable assistant to the community of scholars.

The librarian can help you get the knack of using certain reference works and the card catalogue, once you have tried to use these on your own. But do not expect the librarian to look up the topics for you. Pay attention so that you will be able to handle the resources next time by yourself. When you can't find something and your experience in the library is frustrating, don't give up. Consult the librarian, just as you would consult your instructor when the coursework proves too hard to handle. Your instructor and the librarian may often consult each other on what books to order or to place on reserve, on what materials and facilities are needed for a particular course, and on where certain topics and books can be located.

In the library you may find leads to works that are not in the library. The library is not the whole universe of learning, but it does have an inside connection to the rest of that universe. Consult your librarian concerning access to materials not available at your campus. He may be able to obtain them for you by inter-library loan or direct purchase. Though the library staff and your instructor may make certain suggestions for library use, the full responsibility is yours for learning how to properly learn from the existence of the campus library. The library is waiting for you.

Periodicals. *Periodicals*, so called because they appear at periodic intervals, such as monthly, quarterly, and annually, facilitate the rapid dissemination of ideas among scholars in the form of articles. Philosophic articles appearing in journals are usually rather specialized. Their treatment may be intense, of a narrow problem, and in technical language. *Most journal articles in philosophy are not written for the general reader or the student.* Keep this in mind to avoid disappointments. There is little occasion for you as undergraduate to consult such journals. But sometimes an instructor will recommend a particular article to you, especially if you are writing a term paper on the subject. It may be that the instructor wants you to get a taste of current advanced procedures in philosophy.

Reference works. Philosophic *reference works* include encyclopedias, dictionaries, histories, biographies, indices, bibliographies, and directories. It takes some care to make proper use of them and to avoid being misled by them. *Reference works in philosophy do not have the answers*. In other fields, such as history and the natural sciences, you may find the information that answers central problems in the discipline by looking it up in a reference work. Central to philosophic work is reasoning. It is you who must do the thinking whenever you turn to any philosophy book. Reference works in philosophy serve *to* *refer* you to extensive arguments on a problem or author and to clarify *references* made within a text or lecture you are considering.

This consultation should help you get back to the difficulty with greater understanding, or it should set you ahead into fresh reading and consideration of the general area. Reference materials are not the primary materials of philosophy; they can reflect light on the primary materials. Hence, don't think you know the philosophy of Leibniz because you have read an article on him in an encyclopedia, or that you have mastered Utilitarianism because you looked it up in a dictionary. The general article will help you get started on Leibniz by exposing the main features of his work, but you have to examine those features in Leibniz by your own reading if you are to know his philosophy. And once you have a definition of Utilitarianism you have to go back to the context in which you found it discussed to see how it is used, for only in that sense can you master the concept.

Encyclopedia. It is generally inappropriate to do a philosophy term paper on an *encyclopedia article,* for the article itself is a professional term paper reporting and assessing the work of others. In secondary school you may have been trained to regard the encyclopedia as the last word on any subject; if you took the trouble to look up the subject and read the small print in the heavy volume you would have the truth. That will not do for college. You will have to find the truth by exercise of your own intellectual faculties; if there is any last word on a subject of importance it must be formulated by your understanding. A philosophy term paper is not a report but an exploration and assessment. You could write an assessment of an article if you are already knowledgeable concerning its subject matter. In that case your term paper might become a revised or opposed encyclopedia article.

Philosophic encyclopedias contain extensive articles on philosophers, schools of philosophy or *isms*, ideas, important terms, and big problems. You will need time for careful study of the encyclopedia article. But if you are planning to do further work in an area, say Idealism, consulting the article can save you time in the long run. The article can serve you as an introduction to the subject.

Dictionary. If you have less time and are less concerned about further study, a *philosophical dictionary* may be more useful. Its entries will be shorter and they will mostly deal with technical terms or large concepts. Extensive subjects, such as Idealism, will not be treated extensively, and individual philosophers might not be listed. The dictionary should help you get back to your reading and your thinking with greater clarity of understanding.

In philosophic reasoning there is a need for a fine sense of distinction; philosophers can't breathe without making distinctions. You will have to detect these yourself by paying close attention to the argument. Some philosophic usages go against the grain of ordinary usage, others are rather intricate, and many admit of variation from philosopher to philosopher. When you are ill at ease in the presence of such distinctions, when the use of a term puzzles you, when you wonder what variations in meaning have been given an important idea, then turn to the dictionary.

For philosophy the good dictionary habit is not passive dependence on the dictionary to interpret whatever you read or hear, but rather the development of an active care for clarity in reading and thinking on your part such that you do the work of detecting the trouble and then call in the dictionary to help you. Looking up the troublesome point in the dictionary does not suffice to settle the difficulty. The next step is to get back to the context with a sense of the distinction proposed by the reference work. It is up to you to see to it that you have hit upon the sense of the usage in the argument at hand. It is you not the dictionary that must understand.

Dictionaries give the general sense of a word and its principal variations, but what troubles you is the particular use of the word in the specific book or discussion you encounter. Hence, you are obliged to apply, to alter, or to select from what the entry contains. The genuine meaning of the word you are looking up is not in the dictionary; it is in the passage. Each philosopher reserves the right to give his nuance to the key terms of discussion. Seek out this singular sense armed with the general possibilities given in the dictionary. Philosophical dictionaries do not fix the meaning of terms for workers in the discipline as do some lexicons for the natural sciences and the technologies. In philosophy the dictionary does not dictate. (In addition to ch. 5 on philosophical language, see the discussion in ch. 4 of definition in philosophy.)

History. Histories of philosophy can serve you in several ways. Know why you are consulting the volume so that you can profit from consulting it. Most histories of philosophy are composed around individuals or groups of thinkers, in chronological succession. Sometimes several groups working in a common language over a long period within one tradition are treated as a section of the history, e.g., British Empiricism, German Idealism, American Pragmatism. To consult a history of philosophy you do not have to start at the beginning. Indeed, if you read through a history from cover to cover you are no longer using it as a reference work.

Every history of philosophy is open to critical evaluation in terms of its conception of history (problems of sources, influences, movements, emergence and transmittal of ideas), its conception of philosophy, and its accuracy in representing what was thought by philosophers. Thus, you are not likely to get the settled facts, about, say, Berkeley's theory of knowledge, presented in a philosophically neutral way. Histories like all reference books in philosophy are not to be trusted. But they are useful.

You may have studied some area of a philosopher's work and gleaned bits and pieces of his larger contribution. The history can briefly fit together for you the many sides to the thinker's lifetime of philosophizing. The history can sketch for you the thinker's foreground, that is, the current thought and the contemporary controversies that the thinker faced. This clarifies allusions and gives focus to the refutations or revisions advanced by the thinker. The history places the individual philosopher against the background of previous philosophy, showing how his work may address the problems treated by predecessors. And the history will carry the story further, suggesting what subsequent thinkers thought of his work.

What a history book of philosophy should communicate are the continuity and recurrence, the rediscovery and revision, that characterize the work of philosophers over the ages. A chapter in the history of philosophy is not a posthumous portrait of a subject fixed in the past. For philosophy's past may come alive at any moment. The history book of philosophy will also call your attention to other thinkers you were not aware of but who enter into the story of the philosopher you looked up. This might lead you to read in their works either for their own sake or to better appreciate their relation to the original author.

But inherent limitations are to be found in every history of philosophy. One is the chronological organization, which can separate by a dozen chapters a modern philosopher from ancient philosophers from whom he may have received the greatest stimulation. Most history books make it look as if twentieth-century philosophers respond principally to those of the nineteenth century, who in turn pay closest attention to their forerunners in the eighteenth century, and so on back. You should keep in mind that thought can leap across centuries, directly seizing upon the distant past, and may even turn its back on the past to project the future. Another fault in histories is that they smooth over the irregularities in an epoch, a tradition, a movement, or a thinker's career. The guiding effort is to connect everything, leaving no loose ends. But philosophy inevitably leaves loose ends. Hence, there are philosophers who are out of place in their century, and there are books which are out of place in a philosopher's career.

Many histories of philosophy are more histories of philosophers at work than histories of ideas, problems, and methods, so that you can trace the contribution of a person or school but you lose the thread of what happens over time to a single important concept, say causality. Some help may be had by going through the passages listed for causality in the index. This requires patience, for you have to pick up the thread and follow it through the windings of centuries. There are special reference works in the history of ideas.

Biography. You may consult a *biography* to find out about the character, the events, the public and private life of a philosopher. Philosophers have led interesting lives, as well as dull ones. You may wish to indulge your curiosity some time in looking into their non-philosophic careers. Leibniz handled diplomatic missions, Rousseau composed operettas, Radhakrishnan served as President of India, Francis Bacon as Lord Chancellor of England, Anselm as Archbishop of Canterbury. Jaspers was trained as a psychiatrist, John Locke and Maimonides as medical doctors, Spinoza as a lens grinder, Descartes as a military man, Nietzsche as a philologist. Peirce and Marx had to fight off poverty and even starvation. Epictetus was a slave. A significant number of philosophers have been jailed, exiled, or executed. For notable autobiographies of those who have practiced philosophy see works by Augustine, Abelard, Rousseau, Vico, J. S. Mill, Russell, and Sartre. (Consult the Biographical Notes for further information concerning any philosopher mentioned in this book.)

But you must decide whether you are seeking to know the person or the philosophy when you consult a biography. As a philosopher you have not treated a philosophical contribution properly if you merely examine it as the product or testament of a particular person and age. It must be assessed in terms of what it aims at, namely truth. Philosophical biographies may give precious little attention to the inner person, taking instead the manifest thought of the individual as the subject for treatment. This might be called intellectual biography. The origins, development, and various extensions of a philosopher's thinking in all branches of philosophy will then constitute the biographical entry.

Inherently dubious in a biographical approach is the operating assumption that there is a development in the person's philosophy whereby some works are merely preliminary stages and others the truly mature form of his thinking. Some philosophers may not "develop." What they write at every age may be equally mature. There may be little connection between the works of a thinker at one age and those of his succeeding years, just as there is not necessarily a connection between a thinker's work in the several branches of philosophy.

Reading a brief biography of a philosopher can suggest to you what unity and diversity there is to his work. You can figure out what works to follow up in your own reading. For instance, if you are having trouble with Berkeley's *Principles of Human Knowledge* (1710), you will discover that in 1713 he published *Three Dialogues* with the aim of making his principles easier to grasp. Biographical information can also clarify for you the state of the text you have at hand. If you have been reading a selection from Lenin's treatise on *State and Revolution* (1918), you may discover that it was written in hiding and was never to be completed because Lenin found himself preoccupied with overthrowing the State: "It is more pleasant and useful to go through the 'experience of the revolution' than to write about it." [V. I. Lenin, *State and Revolution* (New York: International Publishers, "Little Lenin Library," 1943), "Postscript to the First Edition," p. 101.]

Index and bibliography. There are *bibliographic indices* in philosophy that can help you locate treatments of an idea, a philosopher, or a movement for further consultation or reading. You can use the index in a pinch when you can't locate anything substantial on a special topic in an encyclopedia or dictionary. And you can turn to the listings when you are curious about the broadest scope of treatment given to the subject. The index will include the unusual alongside the ordinary, and there will be no indication of merit. The index leads you to other works which themselves may lead you to more appropriate materials. Its weaknesses are that it will list more than you can handle in the little time you have and that it will not give you indications as to where to begin.

Specialized *bibliographies* in philosophy can be quite helpful if they are selective and annotated. They serve as a guidebook to the available literature.

Directory. *Directories in philosophy* contain varied information about professional activities in the discipline. They will include such things as the specialties of philosophy instructors, including those at your school, the nature of graduate programs, the availability of fellowships, as well as listings of journals and scholarly associations. If you are interested in graduate work in philosophy a directory can be quite informative.

Mixed reference work. Several kinds of philosophic reference work have been distinguished here in theory, but in practice you are likely to find volumes that are *intermediary* or that *combine* the different kinds in varying proportions. Thus, some dictionaries have extensive articles on big subjects that are akin to an encyclopedia treatment, and the encyclopedia may have a few short dictionary entries. The great eighteenth-century reference work edited by Diderot and D'Alembert in France was called *Encyclopedia, or Systematic Dictionary.* Philosophical biographies may be found in the encyclopedia and they may be introduced throughout a history of philosophy. Biography and encyclopedia should have select bibliographical listings. A cross-reference aid is found in the back of most of these reference works in the form of an index. Of all these kinds of helpful material the encyclopedia is likely to combine most, whence its great size, and a bibliography may be the shortest and simplest reference tool.

General reference. While there are special reference works in philosophy, there are also *general reference works* and works in other fields, including social science, religion, and Oriental studies, which can help you in the same ways. The general works will give you broader treatments that can increase your understanding, though they may be lacking in philosophical precision. General references will also supply you with a lot of information that has nothing to do with your work in philosophy but is biographical, historical, or literary. No matter how distinguished or imposing the reference work, it is still you who are responsible for getting something of philosophical assistance from it. That's not easy. The myth is that the bigger the book you look something up in the less thinking you have to do. Don't believe it. The Greeks had a saying: "Big book: big evil." When you look up anything to help in your philosophical work you can't escape more philosophical work.

Notice that the types of reference material available in the library for a problem may already be present in reduced form in your textbook. Indeed, this may explain why philosophy textbooks are usually very thick and fairly expensive. They may be portable libraries. Begin to think of all the books you encounter as embodying features of the library. Each book has possible reference value in addition to the value of its content. The joke among scholars is that they buy books not for the content but for the footnotes and bibliographies.

Bibliography

1. Library research

Bertman, Martin A. *Research Guide in Philosophy* (Morristown, N.J.: General Learning Press, 1974). Outlines the Library of Congress and Dewey Decimal classification systems in philosophy.

De George, Richard T. *A Guide to Philosophical Bibliography and Research* (New York: Appleton-Century-Crofts, "The Century Philosophy Series," 1971). Very useful guide to many kinds of reference materials. Indicates standard editions of authors.

2. Encyclopedias

Encyclopædia Britannica, 24 vol. (Chicago: Encyclopædia Britannica, 14th ed., 1929). Perhaps the world's leading reference work. Utilizes traditional alphabetical arrangement. The 15th ed., 1974, in 30 volumes, is reorganized as a *Micropædia* with short factual articles, a *Macropædia* with long articles for in-depth study, and a *Propædia* which is an access guide to the entire work.

Encyclopedia of Philosophy, ed. Paul Edwards, 8 vol. (New York: Macmillan, 1967). The most comprehensive reference work in philosophy. Articles by more than 500 contributors on philosophers, branches, and terms. Extensive bibliographies.

Encyclopædia of Religion and Ethics, ed. James Hastings, 12 vol. plus index vol. (New York: Scribner's, 1971). An older (originally 1908–1926) yet reliable work with extensive articles.

Wiener, Philip P. (ed.). *Dictionary of the History of Ideas: Studies of Selected Pivotal Ideas*, 4 vol. (New York: Scribner's, 1973). Surveys of ideas in philosophy as well as other intellectual disciplines.

3. Dictionaries

Random House Dictionary of the English Language, ed. Jess Stein (New York: Random House, 1967). A fine work. Contains a section on foreign languages.

Baldwin, James Mark (ed.). *Dictionary of Philosophy and Psychology*, 4 vol. (Gloucester, Mass.: Peter Smith, 2nd ed., 1957). Originally published in 1901–1905 and still useful. Indicates equivalents of terms in various languages.

Runes, Dagobert D. (ed.). *Dictionary of Philosophy* (Paterson, N.J.: Littlefield, Adams, "New Students Outline Series," 15th ed., 1964). Brief, useful, signed entries on a wide range of problems and terms, including non-Western materials. Poorly printed.

4. Histories

Bréhier, Emile. *The History of Philosophy*, trans. Joseph Thomas and Wade Baskin, 7 vol. (Chicago: University of Chicago Press,

"Phoenix Books," 1963–1969). Monumental and detailed study by outstanding French scholar.

Burnet, John. *Early Greek Philosophy* (Cleveland: World Publishing, "Meridian Books," 4th ed., 1962). A classic. Replete with translations of texts.

Copleston, Frederick, S.J. *A History of Philosophy*, 8 vol., published as 15 (New York: Doubleday, "Image Books," rev. ed., 1962–1966).

Ferm, Vergilius (ed.). *A History of Philosophical Systems* (New York: Philosophical Library, 1950). Useful survey articles on epochs, schools, and branches of philosophy, Eastern as well as Western.

Gilson, Etienne. *History of Christian Philosophy in the Middle Ages* (New York: Random House, 1955).

Klibansky, Raymond (ed.). *Contemporary Philosophy*, 4 vol. (Florence: La Nuova Italia Editrice, 1970). A survey of the current status of work in philosophy by an impressive list of international contributors.

Radhakrishnan, Sarvepalli (ed.). *History of Philosophy: Eastern and Western*, 2 vol. (London: Allen and Unwin, 1952–1953).

Schneider, Herbert W. *A History of American Philosophy* (New York: Columbia University Press, 2nd ed., 1963).

Note: See works listed on history of philosophy in ch. 2.

5. Biographies

Diogenes Laërtius. *Lives of Eminent Philosophers*, with trans. by R. D. Hicks, 2 vol. (Cambridge, Mass.: Harvard University Press, "Loeb Classical Library," 1958–1959). Anecdotes and information about the Greek philosophers.

Tomlin, E. W. F. *The Great Philosophers: The Western World* (New York: A. A. Wyn, 1952). Illustrated.

6. Indices and bibliographies

Bibliography of Philosophy, quarterly, 1937– . Abstracts and notices of philosophical books.

The Great Ideas : A Syntopicon of Great Books of the Western World, ed. Mortimer J. Adler, 2 vol., Volumes II and III of *Great Books of the Western World* (Chicago: Encyclopædia Britannica, 1952). A valuable set of surveys of 102 great ideas, with index to their location in some 50 volumes of great books, and additional bibliographies.

McLean, George F., O.M.I. *Philosophy in the 20th Century: Catholic and Christian*, 2 vol. (New York: Frederick Ungar, 1967). Vol. I is *An Annotated Bibliography of Philosophy in Catholic Thought: 1900–1964*. Very helpful. The brief annotations include designation of the level of readership.

Matczak, Sebastian A. *Philosophy: A Select Classified Bibliography of Ethics, Economics, Law, Politics, Sociology* (Louvain: Nauwelaerts,

"Philosophical Questions Series," 1970). Well organized to help the reader choose material on epochs, theories, and problems.

Philosopher's Index, quarterly, 1967–   . Contains abstracts of articles.

Note: See Bertman and De George under *Library research* above.

7. *Directories*

Directory of American Philosophers: 1976–1977, ed. Archie J. Bahm (Bowling Green, Ohio: Philosophy Documentation Center, 8th ed., 1976). Revised periodically. Contains information on journals, fellowships, societies, as well as an institutional listing of philosophers in the United States and Canada.

Biographical Notes

Abelard (or Abailard), Peter. Born 1079 in Le Pallet, France. Controversial lecturer in Paris. Important dialectician (*Yes and No, Dialectica*). Celebrated for love affair with Héloïse (*History of My Misfortunes*). His tempestuous career ended with death in 1142.

Adler, Mortimer J. Born 1902 in New York. Distinguished educator, editor, historian of ideas, and Neo-Thomist philosopher. A leader of the Great Books movement in America and planner of the new *Encyclopædia Britannica*. *The Idea of Freedom* (1958).

Anselm. Born 1033 in Aosta, Piedmont. St. Anselm served as Archbishop of Canterbury. Celebrated for what has been called the ontological proof of God's existence (*Proslogium*). Died 1109.

Aquinas, Thomas. Born *c.* 1225 in Roccasecca, Italy. Student of Albert the Great. Celebrated lecturer at Rome and other universities. Chided as a "dumb ox," he was probably the greatest mind of Scholasticism. His *Summa Theologica* harmonized Aristotelianism and Christianity. St. Thomas was known as the Angelic Doctor. Stricken ill on a journey, he died while composing a commentary on the Song of Songs, 1274.

Aristotle. Born 384 B.C. in Stagira, Thrace. Studied under Plato. Tutor of Alexander the Great. Founded his own school, the Lyceum, in Athens. His universal intelligence produced pioneering work on the dissection of animals and the analysis of constitutions. In addition, he wrote treatises on logic, poetics, rhetoric, physics, metaphysics, and ethics. Upon the death of Alexander, Aristotle was obliged to flee Athens. Honored in the Middle Ages as "The Philosopher" and "the master of those who know" (Dante). Died 322 B.C.

Augustine (Aurelius Augustinus). Born 354 near Carthage, North Africa. Taught rhetoric in Rome and Milan. After sowing his wild oats, the pagan Augustine converted to Christianity (*Confessions*). St. Augustine tried to harmonize Platonism and Christianity, and to settle doctrinal disputes within Christianity. *The City of God*. Bishop of Hippo in North Africa, he died while the town was under siege by the Vandals, 430.

Ayer, Alfred Jules. Born 1910 in London. Helped introduce Logical Positivism into the English-speaking world (*Language, Truth and*

Logic, 1936?). Professor at Oxford, Sir Alfred is the author of important works in epistemology (*The Problem of Knowledge*, 1956).

Bacon, Francis. Born 1561 in London. Trained as a lawyer, he climbed "the winding stair of fortune" to the post of Lord Chancellor of England. Dismissed and fined for taking bribes. A great force within the Renaissance movement for the advancement of learning (see his work by this title, 1605). Author of *Essays* and a utopia, *The New Atlantis* (1624). Called for the proper exercise of experimental method. He died from a cold contracted while testing the preservative powers of freezing, which involved stuffing a chicken with snow, 1626.

Baumgarten, Alexander G. Born 1714 in Berlin. Taught at Frankfurt-an-der-Oder. His *Aesthetica* (1750) was the pioneering work in what has since been called aesthetics. Died 1762.

Bergson, Henri. Born 1859 in Paris. Philosopher of the life force. Lecturer at the Collège de France in Paris. Recipient of Nobel Prize for Literature (1927). *Creative Evolution* (1907), *Two Sources of Morality and Religion* (1932). Bergson died at 81 after having waited in line in the chilly weather to register as a Jew under the Fascist régime in Paris, 1941.

Berkeley (pronounced "barkly"), George. Born 1685 in Dysert, Ireland. Ingenious theorist who argued for Immaterialism, i. e. things are ideas. Traveled to Rhode Island. Served as Anglican Bishop of Cloyne, Ireland. *Principles of Human Knowledge* (1710), *Three Dialogues* (1713). Died 1753.

Blanshard, Brand. Born 1892 in Fredericksburg, Ohio. Distinguished philosopher of Idealism. Taught at Swarthmore and Yale. *The Nature of Thought* (1939).

Buber, Martin. Born 1878 in Vienna. Profound interpreter of Judaism. Editor, translator, philosopher. Explored the dialogical principle of I and Thou (see his work by this title, 1922). A Zionist, Buber settled in Jerusalem in 1938, where he taught at the Hebrew University. Died 1965.

Carnap, Rudolf. Born 1891 in Ronsdorf, Germany. Student of Frege. A leader of the Vienna Circle of philosophers and scientists. Outstanding Logical Positivist. Emigrated to the United States in 1935. *The Logical Syntax of Language* (1934), *Meaning and Necessity* (1947). Died 1970.

Comte, Auguste. Born 1798 in Montpellier, France. Secretary to Saint-Simon. Founder of Positivism, a new organization and methodology for the sciences. Pioneer in the science of society, for which he coined the name "sociology." Uncompromisingly dull stylist. *Course of Positive Philosophy* (1839–1842). Died 1857.

Condorcet, (Marie Jean de Caritat) Marquis de. Born 1743 in Ribemont, France. Mathematician and philosopher. Early participant in the French Revolution, he subsequently was condemned by the revolutionary Convention. He wrote his masterpiece, *Outline of an*

Historical Portrait of the Progress of the Human Mind, in hiding
shortly before his capture and death in prison, 1794.

Confucius. Born *c.* 551 B.C. in the State of Lu, China. One of China's
great humanistic sages. Editor and teacher of the classics, he traveled throughout the Chinese States seeking a virtuous ruler. Confucius said that if he managed to study for 50 years he might be
free of great mistakes (*Analects*, VII:16). Died 479 B.C.

Croce, Benedetto. Born 1866 in Pescasseroli, Italy. Worked principally in Naples. His pursuit of a philosophy of spirit led to outstanding contributions in aesthetics, philosophy of history, and
theory of culture. Served in the Italian Senate and Cabinet. Remained in Italy during the Fascist reign and was its outspoken op-
ponent. Died 1952.

D'Alembert, Jean le Rond. Born 1717 in Paris and abandoned on the
doorstep of a church. Mathematician, *philosophe*, and early collaborator with Diderot on the French *Encyclopedia* (*Preliminary Discourse*, 1751). Died 1783.

Darwin, Charles R. Born 1809 in Shrewsbury, England. His theory
of evolution set forth in *The Origin of Species* (1859) revolutionized
biology as well as man's self-conception. Worked for 20 years,
including travels around the world, to amass the observations that
supported the theory. Died 1882.

Democritus. Born 460 B.C. in Abdera, Thrace. Propounded the
atomic theory of matter. Sought the truth in clear and distinct sen-
sory impressions. Died 370 B.C.

Descartes, René. Born 1596 in La Haye, France. Retired from military service in middle age to pursue philosophical and scientific interests in Holland. Troubled by doubts, he sought certainty in
clear and distinct ideas. His *Cogito* argument placed metaphysics
on a new Rationalist foundation and his method contributed to the
deductive advancement of the sciences. Inventor of analytic geometry. *Discourse of Method* (1637), *Meditations* (1641). Died from the
effects of tutoring Queen Christina of Sweden in the chill early
mornings of Stockholm, 1650.

Dewey, John. Born 1859 in Burlington, Vt. Influential teacher at
University of Michigan, University of Chicago, and Columbia. A
towering contributor to education, psychology, and philosophy.
Dewey called his brand of Pragmatism "instrumentalism," and
with it he explored the richness of human experience. *Human Nature and Conduct* (1922), *Experience and Nature* (1925), *Art as Experience* (1934). Died 1952.

Diderot, Denis. Born 1713 in Langres, France. Brilliant Parisian man
of letters. Author of satires, tales, art criticism, and articles for the
Encyclopedia, which he edited. *Rameau's Nephew, D'Alembert's Dream,
Jacques the Fatalist* (all written in the 1760s and 1770s). Traveled to
Russia to give lessons to Catherine the Great. Died 1784.

Diogenes Laërtius. Active in the third century. Author of collection of anecdotes concerning the Greek thinkers, *Lives of Eminent Philosophers*. Of his own life nothing is known.

Diogenes of Sinope. Born 412 B.C. in Asia Minor. Active in Athens. Celebrated Cynic (Gr.: "dog-like"). Reputed to have lived in a tub and searched by day with a lantern for an honest man. When Alexander the Great magnanimously offered to fulfill anything he wished, Diogenes replied: "Get out of my light!" No extant writings. Died 323 B.C.

Epictetus. Born a slave *c.* 50 in Hierapolis, Asia Minor. Led a Stoic life and was eventually emancipated. Dictated his views in Greek to Arrianus (*Discourses, Manual*). Banished from Rome and settled in Epirus. Died *c.* 130.

Euclid. Born *c.* 335 B.C. Probably studied with the Platonists in Athens. Founded a school in Alexandria. The Thirteen Books of Euclid's *Elements* are still used in the teaching of plane geometry in public schools. He also wrote *Optics*. Died 275 B.C.

Freud, Sigmund. Born 1856 in Freiberg, Moravia. Received medical training in Paris and Vienna. Experimented with cocaine. Discovered the method of dream interpretation. Exposed the Œdipus Complex. Created the science of Psychoanalysis. Recipient of the Goethe Prize for Literature (1930). *The Interpretation of Dreams* (1900), *A General Introduction to Psychoanalysis* (1915–1917), *Civilization and Its Discontents* (1929). Fled the Nazi régime in Vienna and died shortly after in London, 1939.

Gandhi, Mohandas K. Born 1869 in Porbandar, India. Trained in London as a lawyer, this gentle Hindu went to South Africa to defend Indian interests. Discovered the nonviolent practice of active resistance, which he termed "satyagraha" (*Satyagraha in South Africa*, 1928). Brought this method of universal love to India to secure its independence from Britain. Called Mahatma, "great soul," he once confessed that he had not yet learned to love snakes. Assassinated by a fanatic, 1948.

Hegel, Georg Wilhelm Friedrich. Born 1770 in Stuttgart, Germany. Starting from Kant's work, he developed his own comprehensive version of Idealism as historical process. Celebrated lecturer in the Universities of Jena, Heidelberg, and Berlin; his lectures and notes were published on the philosophy of art, of history, and of politics. Died 1831.

Heidegger, Martin. Born 1889 in Messkirch, Germany. Student of Husserl. The leading Existentialist philosopher in the German language. *Being and Time* (1927), *What Is Metaphysics?* (1929). Praised Nazi ideals in 1933 as Rector of the University of Freiburg. Died 1976.

Heisenberg, Werner. Born 1901 in Würzburg, Germany. Outstanding physicist. Theorist of quantum mechanics. Recipient of Nobel Prize (1932). Assigned to the German atomic bomb project during the Second World War, he sidetracked its development. Died 1976.

Heraclitus. Born *c.* 530 B.C. in Ephesus, Asia Minor. The "dark one" made cryptic and provocative statements about the process and flux of reality, such as "You can't step twice into the same stream." Died *c.* 475 B.C.

Hobbes, Thomas. Born prematurely in 1588 in Malmesbury, England, at the time of the Spanish Armada. Secretary to Francis Bacon. Extended travels and sojourns abroad, including Paris. Tutor of the future Charles II of England. His masterpiece, *Leviathan* (1651), and other political writings caused enormous controversy and gave rise to the pejorative term "Hobbist," meaning one attached to authoritarian principles. An ardent mathematician, Hobbes believed he had solved the squaring of the circle. Translated Homer at 86. Died 1679.

Hume, David. Born 1711 in Edinburgh, Scotland. Published his masterpiece, *A Treatise of Human Nature* (1739–1740), in his twenties, but it "fell dead-born from the press." Turned down for a university post at Edinburgh because of his skepticism in religious matters. Historian and essayist, as well as author of *Enquiries* into human understanding and morals. This judgment of his character is from his autobiographical sketch (1777): "I was, I say, a man of mild dispositions, of command of temper, of an open, social, and cheerful humour, capable of attachment, but little susceptible of enmity, and of great moderation in all my passions." Died 1776.

Husserl, Edmund. Born 1859 in Prossnitz, Moravia. Student of Brentano. Turned from his early work on pure logic to the rigorous science of pure subjectivity, which he called Phenomenology. *Ideas* (1913), *Cartesian Meditations* (1931). Taught at Halle, Göttingen, and Freiburg, Germany. Forbidden to engage in further academic activities by the Nazis, he died in 1938.

James, William. Born 1842 in New York. Educated in Europe and America, as was his brother the novelist Henry. Received medical training. Pioneer psychologist (*The Principles of Psychology*, 1890). Taught at Harvard. Made "Pragmatism" a household word (*Pragmatism: A New Name for Some Old Ways of Thinking*, 1907). Died 1910.

Jaspers, Karl. Born 1883 in Oldenburg, Germany. Student of Max Weber. Trained as a psychiatrist, he turned to philosophical problems of Existentialism and culture. *Reason and Existence* (1935), *The Future of Mankind* (1957). Died 1969.

Jesus of Nazareth. Born *c.* 5 B.C. in Palestine. Jewish teacher who advocated a new commandment of universal love. Preached in Aramaic. No extant writings. Revered by Christianity as the Messiah or Christ and the Son of God. Respected by Islam as a prophet.

Crucified outside of Jerusalem by the Roman provincial government, 29 A.D.

John of Salisbury. Born 1115 in Wiltshire, England. Student of Abelard. Secretary to Thomas à Becket, whose murder he witnessed. Bishop of Chartres. Author of Medieval classics on politics (*The Policraticus*) and education (*The Metalogicon*). Died 1180.

Kant, Immanuel. Born 1724 in Königsberg, East Prussia. Awakened from his "dogmatic şlumbers" by a study of Hume, he brought about a Copernican Revolution in Philosophy by turning critical inquiry upon the knowing, acting, and judging subject. Best known for his three *Critiques:* of *Pure Reason* (1781), of *Practical Reason* (1788), and of *Judgment* (1790). As the motto of the Enlightenment he proclaimed *Sapere aude!* "Dare to know!" His habits were so regular that townspeople are said by Heine to have set their watches by his appearances in Königsberg, where he spent his life teaching. His student, Herder, said of Kant: "He was indifferent to nothing worth knowing" (trans. Lewis White Beck). Died 1804.

Kierkegaard, Søren. Born 1813 in Copenhagen. A tortured man who explored the secrets of fear, loneliness, irony, and faith, often in pseudonymous and involuted works, which remain the greatest achievements of Danish literature. *Either/Or* (1843), *Fear and Trembling* (1843), *The Concept of Dread* (1844). Rebelled against Hegelianism and systematic philosophy. A hunchback, he is one of the giants of early Existentialism. Unhappy in love, alienated by society, this lost soul died at 42 in 1855.

Lao Tzu. Born *c.* 604 B.C. in China. The author of the classic work of Taoism, the *Tao-te Ching*. Supposedly a contemporary of Confucius; all that we know of him is legendary, including the story that a gatekeeper obliged him to write the *Tao-te Ching* before letting him cross the border.

Leibniz, Gottfried Wilhelm. Born 1646 in Leipzig, Germany. Settled in Hanover. Brilliant thinker who invented the differential calculus and extended the philosophy of Rationalism. Cosmopolitan, he wrote in French and Latin and worked for the political and religious reconciliation of Europe. *New Essays on Human Understanding* (written 1703 as a reply to Locke), *Monadology* (1714). Died 1716.

Locke, John. Born 1632 in Wrington, England. Trained as a medical doctor, Locke was obliged to flee to Holland because of his politics. Returned to England in 1689 upon the success of the Glorious Revolution. The next year published his two great works, the *Essay Concerning Human Understanding* and *Two Treatises of Government*. Locke was a patron saint of the Enlightenment, especially in America. Died 1704.

Lucretius (Titus Lucretius Carus). Born *c.* 99 B.C. in Rome. Little is known of his life. According to St. Jerome, he went mad and killed himself. His *On the Nature of Things* is a masterful Latin poem that applies the materialistic doctrines of Epicurus to nature, man, and society. Died 55 B.C.

Maimonides (Moses ben Maimon). Born 1143 in Córdoba, Spain. Jewish scholar and medical doctor. Wrote in Arabic. Lived in Spain and North Africa. *Guide for the Perplexed.* Died 1204 in Cairo.

Marx, Karl. Born 1818 in Trier, Germany. His early studies in philosophy led him "to turn Hegel rightside up," putting the dialectical development of history on a new materialistic footing. His *Communist Manifesto* (1848), written with his lifelong collaborator Friedrich Engels, shocked Europe into awareness of the "specter of Communism." A prolific writer, he did his research for the new science of history in the reading room of the British Museum. *Capital* (1867). Marx, whose ideas may have changed the lives of more people on earth than anyone since Jesus, lived in bitter poverty in London, where he died in 1883.

Mill, John Stuart. Born 1806 in London. Reared according to Benthamite views by his father, the philosopher James Mill, John Stuart learned Greek at age 3, Latin at 8, and had a nervous breakdown at 20. He became a leader of Utilitarianism, founded on the greatest happiness principle. Worked in the East India Company and served briefly in Parliament. Champion of the rights and liberty of men and women. *System of Logic* (1843), *On Liberty* (1859), *Utilitarianism* (1861). Died in Avignon, France, where he had retired, 1873.

Montaigne, Michel de. Born 1533 near Bordeaux, France. Trained as a lawyer. Served as a municipal and regional official. One of the giants of the Renaissance, Montaigne composed stoic and humane reflections on many subjects (*Essays*, 1580). His motto: *Que sais-je?* "What do I know?" Died 1592.

Nietzsche, Friedrich. Born 1844 in Röcken, Prussia. A student of languages, he became a professor in Basel, Switzerland. He wrote disturbing attacks on everything valued in Western civilization: *Thus Spoke Zarathustra* (1882), *Beyond Good and Evil* (1886), *The Genealogy of Morals* (1887). A great master of the German language, he wrote with the powers of poet and prophet. Warned: "We are unknown to ourselves, we knowers." Called for the creation of a strong noble man (*der Übermensch*). A highly sensitive man, passionate but a loner, always weak in health, Nietzsche lost his sanity a dozen years before his death in 1900.

Ortega y Gasset, José. Born 1883 in Madrid. Active in Spanish republicanism. Exiled during the Civil War. Lived in Argentina. Editor and essayist, Ortega is the giant of Spanish letters in the twentieth century. *The Rebellion of the Masses* (1930) is his best known work. Died 1955.

Pascal, Blaise. Born 1623 in Clermont-Ferrand, France. Brilliant mathematician, polemicist, and analyst of Christian faith. Invented calculating machine. Proclaimed "The heart has its reasons of which the reason knows naught" (*Pensées*, no. 703). Associated with the Port-Royal Jansenists in Paris. His major work, *Penséees* (Thoughts), intended as an Apology for Christianity, was left unfinished at his death in 1662.

Peirce (pronounced "purse"), Charles Sanders. Born 1839 in Cambridge, Mass. Original and stimulating thinker, founder of Pragmatism. Never completed a book and never succeeded in holding onto a university job. Worked for the U.S. Coast and Geodetic Survey. Suffered great personal hardships. Died at his home in Milford, Pa., 1914.

Plato. Born *c.* 427 B.C. in Athens. Student of Socrates and author of many Socratic dialogues. Founded a school in Athens in the "Groves of Academe": the Academy. Traveled to Sicily. Taught a theory of Ideas with a fully developed and integrated account of nature, man, society, knowledge, and art. Portrayed the ideal society in *The Republic*. Whitehead remarked that all Western philosophy is merely footnotes to Plato. Died 347 B.C.

Plekhanov, George V. Born 1856 in Tambov, Russia. Lived as exile in Geneva most of his life. Regarded as the father of Russian Marxism. *The Role of the Individual in History* (1898), *Fundamental Problems of Marxism* (1908). Died 1918 in Finland.

Protagoras. Born *c.* 490 B.C. in Abdera, Thrace. A celebrated Sophist, he visited Athens to teach politics and persuasion (see Plato, *Protagoras*). He asserted the relativity of knowledge. Banished from Athens for impiety. Died *c.* 421 B.C.

Pythagoras. Born *c.* 572 B.C. on Samos in the Aegean Sea. Mathematician and speculator upon the foundations of the universe, which he took to be numbers. A theorem in geometry is named after him. Founded a philosophical and religious movement in southern Italy. He is reputed to have listened to the "music of the celestial spheres" while sitting upon the shore. Died 497 B.C.

Radhakrishnan, Sarvepalli. Born 1888 in Tiruttani, south India. A Hindu scholar, master of Indian and Western philosophies and religions. As editor, translator, diplomat, and philosopher of religion he did much to bring East and West into fruitful contact. *An Idealist View of Life* (1932), *Eastern Religions and Western Thought* (1939). Served as delegate to UNESCO, ambassador to the Soviet Union, Vice-President and then President of India. Died 1975.

Rousseau, Jean-Jacques. Born 1712 in Geneva. Led a tumultuous life. Pursued by fears of persecution—and by persecutors. Quarreled with Voltaire, Hume, D'Alembert, Diderot. Abandoned his five children to a foundling home. Wrote works of romantic literature (*The New Héloïse*, 1761), startling autobiographic works (*Confessions*, 1782), and influential works in political theory (*The Social Contract*,

1762). Settled in a rustic cottage at Ermenonville, France, which had a trap door for him to escape visitors. Died 1778.

Russell, Bertrand. Born 1872 in Trelleck, Wales. Collaborated with Whitehead on *Principia Mathematica* (1910–1913), the classic of symbolic logic. In addition to theory of knowledge, logic, and philosophy of science, he wrote on social and political problems. Author of scores of books, remarkable for their clarity of expression (*Power*, 1938, *A History of Western Philosophy*, 1945, *Has Man a Future?* 1961). Recipient of Nobel Prize for Literature (1950). Dismissed from his post at Cambridge University because of his pacifist views, forbidden to teach at City College of New York because of his moral ideas. Spoke out and acted against warfare from the Boer War to the Vietnam War. Eloquent champion for the life of reason and kindness in a world of suffering and violence. Died in his 98th year in 1970.

Santayana, George. Born 1863 in Madrid and remained a Spanish subject throughout his life. Came to America at 9. Taught at Harvard but resigned to live in Europe. Poet and novelist as well as philosopher, he reminded us, "It is wisdom to believe the heart." *The Life of Reason* (1905–1906), *Realms of Being* (1927–1940). Died 1952 in Italy.

Sartre, Jean-Paul. Born 1905 in Paris. Editor, novelist and playwright, Existentialist philosopher, and leader of reform causes. Companion of Simone de Beauvoir. *Nausea* (1938), *Being and Nothingness* (1943), *Critique of Dialectical Reasoning* (1960). Sartre takes his stand on behalf of human freedom and responsibility. Declined the Nobel Prize for Literature (1964).

Schopenhauer, Arthur. Born 1788 in Danzig, Poland. Traveled through Europe as a youth. University education in Germany. Philosopher of the will (*The World as Will and Representation*, 1819). Notorious for his pessimism. Schopenhauer scheduled his lectures at the University of Berlin for the same hours as Hegel. He lost his audience and soon after returned to private life. Died 1860.

Socrates. Born *c.* 469 B.C. in Athens. Called the wisest of men by the Delphic Oracle, Socrates thought it was because he was aware of his own ignorance. Spent his time in public places questioning people who might know about justice, virtue, piety. For this he was brought to trial as a subversive. His reply to plea bargaining when offered his life if he would keep quiet: "The unexamined life is not worth living" (Plato, *Apology*, 38). No extant writings. For more than two thousand years Socrates has served as model of the philosophic life. Condemned to death, he drank the prescribed poison, 399 B.C.

Spinoza, Baruch (or Benedict) de. Born 1632 in Amsterdam into a family of Portuguese Jews. Worked out the implications of Cartesian deductive reasoning in ethics (*Ethics*, 1677) and politics

(*Theologico-Political Treatise*, 1670). This "God-intoxicated man" (Novalis) was excommunicated by the Synagogue of Amsterdam as a heretic and forced to leave town. Made his living polishing lenses. Declined a professorship at Heidelberg in order to retain his independence. Died 1677.

Thales. Born *c.* 624 B.C. in Miletus, Asia Minor. One of the Seven Wise Men and early Greek seekers for the principle of things, which he found to be water. No extant writings. Supposed to have predicted eclipses and rumored to have tumbled into a well while looking at the stars. Died *c.* 550 B.C.

Thoreau, Henry David. Born 1817 in Concord, Mass. Transcendentalist and friend of the American movement's leader, Ralph Waldo Emerson. Went off to live in the woods at Walden Pond (*Walden*, 1854). Spent a night in jail for refusal to pay taxes that supported unjust war and slavery. Spoke of the righteous man as a "majority of one" ("Civil Disobedience," 1849). Died 1862.

Tillich, Paul. Born 1886 in Starzeddel, Prussia. Emigrated to the United States in 1933. One of the greatest theologians of the twentieth century. *Systematic Theology* (1951–1963), *The Courage to Be* (1952). Died 1965.

Tolstoy, Leo N. Born 1828 in central Russia. One of the world's greatest novelists (*War and Peace*, 1869, *Anna Karenina*, 1877). A profound religious experience led to his works on Christianity (*The Kingdom of God Is within You*, 1890–1893), social obligation (*What then Must We Do?* 1882–1886), and even aesthetic theory (*What Is Art?* 1897–1898). Excommunicated by the Russian Orthodox Church. Many of his works were banned by the Czarist government. A Count, he decided to live the simple life of a peasant on his own estate. Died 1910.

Unamuno y Jugo, Miguel de. Born 1864 of Basque origin in Bilbao, Spain. Novelist, essayist, educator. Profound interpreter of the Spanish soul—and of the human soul. Reminded us that even a philosopher is a man of flesh and bone. Served as Rector of the University of Salamanca until dismissed by the Fascist forces. Died while under house arrest, 1936.

Vaihinger, Hans. Born 1852 in Nehren, Germany. Taught at University of Halle. A Kantian philosopher who argued for the role of fictions in thought. *The Philosophy of "As If"* (1911). Died 1933.

Vico, Giambattista. Born 1668 in Naples. One of the great philosophers of culture, proposing a new science (see his work by that title, 1725) for interpreting history, language, art, and philosophy. His work has been widely neglected until recent years. Died 1744.

Voltaire (François Marie Arouet). Born 1694 in Paris. A great success as dramatist, historian, satirist, writer of philosophic tales, and social critic. The most celebrated man of letters of the eighteenth century. Many of his works were banned or burned, and he spent time in the Bastille. His motto: *Écrasez l'infâme!* "Stamp out the infamous one!" i. e. Superstition or Foolish Authority. *Essay on Manners* (1756), *Candide* (1759). Died 1778.

Whitehead, Alfred North. Born 1861 in Ramsgate, England. Distinguished as a mathematician at Cambridge University, he collaborated with Bertrand Russell on the great *Principia Mathematica* (1910–1913). He came to the United States in 1924 to embark upon a second career as philosopher of science and metaphysician. Taught at Harvard. Developed process philosophy in luminous books such as *Process and Reality* (1929) and *Adventures of Ideas* (1933). Died 1947.

William of Occam (or Ockham). Born *c*. 1285 in Surrey, England. Engaged in the theoretical debate on the powers of Church and State. A Nominalist; his "Razor" dispensed with unnecessary terms. *Logical Treatise, Commentary on the Books of Sentences.* Died 1349.

Wittgenstein, Ludwig. Born 1889 in Vienna. Student of Bertrand Russell. While a prisoner of war in World War I he finished the famous *Tractatus* (1921), his only book to be published during his lifetime. Taught at Cambridge. Notes of Wittgenstein's courses are now being published and expounded. *Philosophical Investigations* (1953), *The Blue and Brown Books* (1958). Died 1951.

Zeno of Elea. Born *c*. 490 B.C. in Italy. Student of Parmenides. Celebrated for his paradoxes, including this one: Achilles can never overtake the tortoise who has been given a headstart, since by the time the swift hero reaches the point where the tortoise was, the slow creature has moved on, and so on *ad infinitum*. In other words, motion is impossible. Zeno, however, managed to visit Athens, where he met Socrates. Died 430 B.C.

Handbook Evaluation Form

Those who use this handbook are encouraged to let the author know their opinions of it so that a more serviceable book may be issued in the future.

Mail to:

Mr. Robert Ginsberg
Welcome to Philosophy!
c/o Freeman, Cooper & Company
1736 Stockton Street
San Francisco, CA 94133

Date:
To the Author of *Welcome to Philosophy!*:
I have used your book in conjunction with my study of philosophy, and I want you to know that (*please indicate your candid judgments, comments, complaints, suggestions for improvement, etc.*):

_____

_____

_____

_____

_____

_____

_____

_____

_____

_____

_____

You may/may not (*cross out one*) quote me for publication.

_____